TO

_____

FROM

_____

DATE

_____

Blessed are the pure in heart, for they shall see God.
MATTHEW 5:8 NKJV

FAMILY
Christian Stores®

THE LIVING SERIES

PURITY
FOR *Young*
WOMEN

31 DAILY DEVOTIONS

The quoted ideas expressed in this book (but not scripture verses) are not, in all cases, exact quotations, as some have been edited for clarity and brevity. In all cases, the author has attempted to maintain the speaker's original intent. In some cases, quoted material for this book was obtained from secondary sources, primarily print media. While every effort was made to ensure the accuracy of these sources, the accuracy cannot be guaranteed. For additions, deletions, corrections or clarifications in future editions of this text, please write FAMILY CHRISTIAN STORES.

Scripture quotations are taken from:

The Holy Bible, King James Version

The Holy Bible, New International Version (NIV) Copyright © 1973, 1978, 1984, by International Bible Society. Used by permission of Zondervan Publishing House. All rights reserved.

The Holy Bible, New King James Version (NKJV) Copyright © 1982 by Thomas Nelson, Inc. Used by permission.

The New American Standard Bible®, (NASB) Copyright © 1960, 1962, 1963, 1968, 1971, 1972, 1973, 1975, 1977, 1995 by The Lockman Foundation. Used by permission.

Holy Bible, New Living Translation, (NLT) Copyright © 1996. Used by permission of Tyndale House Publishers, Inc., Wheaton, Illinois 60189. All rights reserved.

The Message (MSG)- This edition issued by contractual arrangement with NavPress, a division of The Navigators, U.S.A. Originally published by NavPress in English as THE MESSAGE: The Bible in Contemporary Language copyright 2002-2003 by Eugene Peterson. All rights reserved.

New Century Version®. (NCV) Copyright © 1987, 1988, 1991 by Word Publishing, a division of Thomas Nelson, Inc. All rights reserved. Used by permission.

The Holman Christian Standard Bible™ (Holman CSB) Copyright © 1999, 2000, 2001 by Holman Bible Publishers. Used by permission.

Cover Design by Kim Russell / Wahoo Designs
Page Layout by Bart Dawson

ISBN-13 978-1-58334-459-0

ISBN-10 1-58334-459-4

Printed in the United States of America

PURITY
FOR *Young*
WOMEN

TABLE OF CONTENTS

INTRODUCTION

As a young woman living in a troubled world, you know how difficult it is to keep your heart pure. Society keeps pumping out messages that encourage you to compromise yourself and betray your values. But these messages are untrue. The real path to contentment and peace is God's path, not society's.

Sometimes it seems that life here in the 21st century has been designed with an overriding purpose in mind: to test—and if possible, to tear down—your character. At almost every turn, you are tempted to follow the wrong role models, to betray your conscience, and to give in to the temptations that are now woven into the fabric of everyday life. If you fall prey to these temptations, you will inevitably disappoint your family, yourself, and your Creator. A far better strategy is to guard your heart by remaining pure.

In your hands, you hold a book that contains 31 devotional readings. During the coming month, please try this experiment: read a chapter each day. If you're already committed to a daily time of worship, this book will enrich that experience. If you are not, the simple act of giving God a few minutes each morning will change the direction and the quality of your life.

This book is intended to remind you of the importance of purity and of God's never-ending love for You. May these pages be a blessing to you, and may you, in turn, be a blessing to those whom God has seen fit to place along your path.

DAY 1

KNOWING GOD

Be still, and know that I am God.
PSALM 46:10 NKJV

YOU WILL LIVE WISELY AND WELL IF . . .
You spend time each day getting to know God.

D o you ever wonder if God is really "right here, right now"? Do you wonder if God hears your prayers, if He understands your feelings, or if He really knows your heart? If so, you're not alone: lots of very faithful Christians have experienced periods of doubt. In fact, some of the biggest heroes in the Bible had plenty of doubts—and so, perhaps, will you. But when you have doubts, remember this: God isn't on a coffee break, and He hasn't moved out of town. God isn't taking a long vacation, and He isn't snoozing on the couch. He's right here, right now, listening to your thoughts and prayers, watching over your every move.

The Bible teaches that a wonderful way to get to know God is simply to be still and listen to Him. But sometimes, you may find it hard to slow down and listen. As the demands of everyday life weigh down upon you, you may be tempted to ignore God's presence or—worse yet—to rebel against His commandments. But, when you quiet yourself and acknowledge His presence, God touches your heart and restores your spirits. So why not let Him do it right now? If you really want to know Him better, silence is a wonderful place to start.

MORE FROM GOD'S WORD

You shall have no other gods before Me.

EXODUS 20:3 NKJV

For it is written, "You shall worship the Lord your God, and Him only you shall serve."

MATTHEW 4:10 NKJV

The one who does not love does not know God, because God is love.

1 JOHN 4:8 HCSB

God is Spirit, and those who worship Him must worship in spirit and truth.

JOHN 4:24 HCSB

Knowing God leads to self-control. Self-control leads to patient endurance, and patient endurance leads to godliness.

2 PETER 1:6 NLT

MORE IDEAS ABOUT
KNOWING GOD

We all need to make time for God. Even Jesus made time to be alone with the Father.

KAY ARTHUR

God wants to be in an intimate relationship with you. He's the God who has orchestrated every event of your life to give you the best chance to get to know Him, so that you can experience the full measure of His love.

BILL HYBELS

Knowing God involves an intimate, personal relationship that is developed over time through prayer and getting answers to prayer, through Bible study and applying its teaching to our lives, through obedience and experiencing the power of God, through moment-by-moment submission to Him that results in a moment-by-moment filling of the Holy Spirit.

ANNE GRAHAM LOTZ

We can seek God and find him! God is knowable, touchable, hearable, seeable, with the mind, the hands, the ears, and eyes of the inner man.

A. W. TOZER

A man's spiritual health is exactly proportional to his love for God.

C. S. LEWIS

It is always springtime in the heart that loves God.

ST. JOHN VIANNEY

Slowly and surely, we learn the great secret of life, which is to know God.

OSWALD CHAMBERS

Here is our opportunity: we cannot see God, but we can see Christ. Christ was not only the Son of God, but He was the Father. Whatever Christ was, that God is.

HANNAH WHITALL SMITH

THE TIP OF THE DAY

Finding time for God takes time . . . and it's up to you to find it. The world is constantly vying for your attention, and sometimes the noise can be deafening. Remember the words of Elisabeth Elliot; she said, "The world is full of noise. Let us learn the art of silence, stillness, and solitude."

THE PRAYER OF THE DAY

Lord, help me to hear Your direction for my life
in the quiet moments of each day. Let everything
that I say and do be in Your perfect will.

Amen

MY THOUGHTS ABOUT
KNOWING GOD

_____

_____

_____

_____

_____

_____

_____

_____

DAY 2

TEMPTATION IS EVERYWHERE, BUT GOD GIVES YOU THE STRENGTH TO BE STRONG

*But remember that the temptations that come into your life
are no different from what others experience. And God is faithful.
He will keep the temptation from becoming so strong that
you can't stand up against it. When you are tempted,
he will show you a way out so that you will not give in to it.*

1 CORINTHIANS 10:13 NLT

YOU WILL LIVE WISELY AND WELL IF . . .
You recognize that temptations are temporary
but God's love is not.

H ave you noticed that this world is filled to the brim with temptations? Unless you've been living the life of a hermit, you've observed that temptations, both great and small, are everywhere.

Some temptations are small; eating a second scoop of ice cream, for example, is tempting, but not very dangerous. Other temptations, however, are not nearly so harmless. The devil is working 24/7, and he's causing pain and heartache in more ways than ever before. Thankfully, in the battle against Satan, we are never alone. God is always with us, and He gives us the power to resist temptation whenever we ask Him for the strength to do so.

In a letter to believers, Peter offered a stern warning: "Your adversary the devil walks about like a roaring lion, seeking whom he may devour" (1 Peter 5:8 NKJV). As Christians, we must take that warning seriously, and we must behave accordingly.

MORE FROM GOD'S WORD

Let us throw off everything that hinders and the sin that so easily entangles, and let us run with perseverance the race marked out for us.

HEBREWS 12:1 NIV

Put on the full armor of God so that you can stand against the tactics of the Devil.

EPHESIANS 6:11 HCSB

Be sober! Be on the alert! Your adversary the Devil is prowling around like a roaring lion, looking for anyone he can devour.

1 PETER 5:8 HCSB

For we do not have a High Priest who cannot sympathize with our weaknesses, but was in all points tempted as we are, yet without sin. Let us therefore come boldly to the throne of grace, that we may obtain mercy and find grace to help in time of need.

HEBREWS 4:15-16 NKJV

Do not be deceived: "Bad company corrupts good morals."

1 CORINTHIANS 15:33 HCSB

MORE IDEAS ABOUT TEMPTATION

Do not fight the temptation in detail. Turn from it. Look ONLY at your Lord. Sing. Read. Work.

AMY CARMICHAEL

Instant intimacy is one of the leading warning signals of a seduction.

BETH MOORE

Our Lord has given us an example of how to overcome the devil's temptations. When He was tempted in the wilderness, He defeated Satan every time by the use of the Bible.

BILLY GRAHAM

Take a really honest look at yourself. Have any old sins begun to take control again? This would be a wonderful time to allow Him to bring fresh order out of longstanding chaos.

CHARLES SWINDOLL

Temptation is not a sin. Even Jesus was tempted. The Lord Jesus gives you the strength needed to resist temptation.

CORRIE TEN BOOM

The Bible teaches us in times of temptation there is one command: Flee! Get away from it, for every struggle against lust using only one's own strength is doomed to failure.

DIETRICH BONHOEFFER

Every time we are tempted in life, it will be by something immediate. It will be something that will suggest to us that we need to postpone the more important for the more urgent.

FRANKLIN GRAHAM

Sin is an allergic reaction to God's law, an irrational anti-God syndrome that drives us to exalt ourselves and steels our heart against devotion and obedience to our Maker.

J. I. PACKER

THE TIP OF THE DAY

At every turn in the road, or so it seems, somebody is trying to tempt you with something. Your job is to steer clear of temptation . . . and to keep steering clear as long as you live. Remember the old saying: "When it comes to temptation, it's easier to stay out than it is to get out."

THE PRAYER OF THE DAY

Lord, temptation is everywhere! Help me turn from it
and to run from it! Let me keep Christ in my heart,
and let me put the devil in his place: far away from me!

Amen

MY THOUGHTS ABOUT
TEMPTATION

_____

_____

_____

_____

_____

_____

_____

DAY 3

YOU'RE INCREDIBLY VALUABLE TO GOD, AND YOU SHOULD BE INCREDIBLY VALUABLE TO YOURSELF

*You're blessed when you're content with just who you are—
no more, no less. That's the moment you find yourselves proud
owners of everything that can't be bought.*

MATTHEW 5:5 MSG

YOU WILL LIVE WISELY AND WELL IF . . .
You recognize that you are a unique, incredibly valuable
human being . . . and if you treat yourself that way.

What are you telling yourself about yourself? When you look in the mirror, are you staring back at your biggest booster or your harshest critic? If you can learn to give yourself the benefit of the doubt—if you can learn how to have constructive conversations with the person you see in the mirror—then your self-respect will tend to take care of itself. But, if you're constantly berating yourself—if you're constantly telling yourself that you can't measure up—then you'll find that self-respect is always in short supply.

Thoughts are intensely powerful things. Your thoughts have the power to lift you up or drag you down; they have the power to energize you or deplete you, to inspire you to greater accomplishments, or to make those accomplishments impossible.

The Bible teaches you to guard your thoughts against things that are hurtful or wrong (Proverbs 4:23). Yet sometimes you'll be tempted to let your thoughts run wild, especially if those thoughts are of the negative variety.

If you've acquired the habit of thinking constructively about yourself and your circumstances, congratulations. But if you're mired in the mental quicksand of overly self-critical thoughts, it's time to change your thoughts . . . and your life.

MORE FROM GOD'S WORD

A devout life does bring wealth, but it's the rich simplicity of being yourself before God.

1 TIMOTHY 6:6 MSG

You made all the delicate, inner parts of my body and knit me together in my mother's womb. Thank you for making me so wonderfully complex! Your workmanship is marvelous—and how well I know it.

PSALM 139:13-14 NLT

My dear children, let's not just talk about love; let's practice real love. This is the only way we'll know we're living truly, living in God's reality. It's also the way to shut down debilitating self-criticism, even when there is something to it. For God is greater than our worried hearts and knows more about us than we do ourselves. And friends, once that's taken care of and we're no longer accusing or condemning ourselves, we're bold and free before God!

1 JOHN 3:18-21 MSG

That is why we can say with confidence, "The Lord is my helper, so I will not be afraid. What can mere mortals do to me?"

HEBREWS 13:6 NLT

MORE IDEAS ABOUT
SELF-ESTEEM

You are valuable just because you exist. Not because of what you do or what you have done, but simply because you are.

MAX LUCADO

If you ever put a price tag on yourself, it would have to read "Jesus" because that is what God paid to save you.

JOSH MCDOWELL

Being loved by Him whose opinion matters most gives us the security to risk loving, too—even loving ourselves.

GLORIA GAITHER

Find satisfaction in him who made you, and only then find satisfaction in yourself as part of his creation.

ST. AUGUSTINE

The Creator has made us each one of a kind. There is nobody else exactly like us, and there never will be. Each of us is his special creation and is alive for a distinctive purpose.

LUCI SWINDOLL

Your self-image need not be permanently damaged by the circumstances of life. It can be recast when there is an infusion of new life in Jesus Christ.

ED YOUNG

Give yourself a gift today: be present with yourself. God is. Enjoy your own personality. God does.

BARBARA JOHNSON

Your core identity—and particularly your perception of it—plays a vital role in determining how you carry yourself in daily life, how much joy you experience, how you treat other people, and how you respond to God.

JOSH MCDOWELL

THE TIP OF THE DAY

Watch what you think. If your inner voice is, in reality, your inner critic, you need to tone down the criticism now. And while you're at it, train yourself to begin thinking thoughts that are more rational, more accepting, and less judgmental.

THE PRAYER OF THE DAY

Dear Lord, keep me mindful that I am a special person,
created by You, loved by You, and saved by Your Son.

Amen

MY THOUGHTS ABOUT
SELF-ESTEEM

_____

_____

_____

_____

_____

_____

_____

DAY 4

PURITY
DAY BY DAY

*Flee also youthful lusts; but pursue righteousness, faith, love, peace
with those who call on the Lord out of a pure heart.*
2 TIMOTHY 2:22 NKJV

YOU WILL LIVE WISELY AND WELL IF . . .
You understand the blessings of purity.

The Bible instructs us to be pure in our motives, our thoughts, and our actions. But the world tries to convince us that purity isn't really very important. The world tries to convince us that immediate pleasure is more important than righteous living, yet nothing could be further from the truth.

Sometimes it's hard to do the right thing, especially if you pay attention to all the messages that the media keeps pumping out. Those messages, which seem to pop up just about everywhere, try to tell you how you should look and how you should behave. The media isn't interested in purity (your purity or its purity). The media is interested in selling you the ideas and products of popular culture. And if you're wise, you won't buy into all those media lies.

Striving for purity isn't a sometimes thing—purity unfolds day by day. It's the result of every good deed, every heartfelt prayer, every kind word, and every sensible thought. Being pure isn't a sprint, it's a marathon. And it's a marathon you can win—and should win.

MORE FROM GOD'S WORD

For God has not called us to impurity, but to sanctification.

1 THESSALONIANS 4:7 HCSB

Even a child is known by his actions, by whether his conduct is pure and right.

PROVERBS 20:11 NIV

Now the goal of our instruction is love from a pure heart, a good conscience, and a sincere faith.

1 TIMOTHY 1:5 HCSB

You should be an example to the believers in speech, in conduct, in love, in faith, in purity.

1 TIMOTHY 4:12 HCSB

Let us draw near with a true heart in full assurance of faith, our hearts sprinkled clean from an evil conscience and our bodies washed in pure water.

HEBREWS 10:22 HCSB

MORE IDEAS ABOUT PURITY AND OBEDIENCE

A life lived in God is not lived on the plane of feelings, but of the will.

ELISABETH ELLIOT

The purity of motive determines the quality of action.

OSWALD CHAMBERS

A life growing in its purity and devotion will be a more prayerful life.

E. M. BOUNDS

It is the Spirit who brings us into ever-deeper, ever-fuller purity of heart.

RICHARD FOSTER

Simplicity reaches out after God; purity discovers and enjoys him.

THOMAS À KEMPIS

Religious activity can never substitute for a heart that is pure before Him.

HENRY BLACKABY

Spiritual truth is discernible only to a pure heart, not to a keen intellect. It is not a question of profundity of intellect, but of purity of heart.

OSWALD CHAMBERS

Those whose hearts are pure are the temples of the Holy Spirit.

LUCI SWINDOLL

THE TIP OF THE DAY

Today, think about the value of a pure and holy life, a life that is pleasing to God. And while you're at it, think about the rewards that will be yours when you do the right thing day in and day out.

THE PRAYER OF THE DAY

Dear Lord, give me pure thoughts and a pure heart.
And, when I am tempted to disobey Your commandments,
keep me mindful that my real blessings
come from You today and forever.
Amen

MY THOUGHTS ABOUT
PURITY AND OBEDIENCE

_____

_____

_____

_____

_____

_____

_____

_____

DAY 5

GOD IS
RIGHT HERE

Draw close to God, and God will draw close to you.

JAMES 4:8 NLT

YOU WILL LIVE WISELY AND WELL IF . . .
You strive to sense God's presence every day.

ince God is everywhere, we are free to sense His presence whenever we take the time to quiet our souls and turn our prayers to Him. But sometimes, amid the incessant demands of everyday life, we turn our thoughts far from God; when we do, we suffer.

Do you set aside quiet moments each day to offer praise to your Creator? As a woman who has received the gift of God's grace, you most certainly should. Silence is a gift that you give to yourself and to God. During these moments of stillness, you will often sense the infinite love and power of your Creator—and He, in turn, will speak directly to your heart.

The familiar words of Psalm 46:10 remind us to "Be still, and know that I am God." When we do so, we encounter the awesome presence of our loving Heavenly Father, and we are comforted in the knowledge that God is not just near. He is here.

MORE FROM GOD'S WORD

No, I will not abandon you as orphans—I will come to you.

JOHN 14:18 NLT

Again, this is God's command: to believe in his personally named Son, Jesus Christ. He told us to love each other, in line with the original command. As we keep his commands, we live deeply and surely in him, and he lives in us. And this is how we experience his deep and abiding presence in us: by the Spirit he gave us.

1 JOHN 3:23-24 MSG

You will seek Me and find Me when you search for Me with all your heart.

JEREMIAH 29:13 HCSB

Let your gentleness be evident to all. The Lord is near.

PHILIPPIANS 4:5 NIV

Where can I go from your Spirit? Where can I flee from your presence? If I go up to the heavens, you are there; if I make my bed in the depths, you are there. If I rise on the wings of the dawn, if I settle on the far side of the sea, even there your hand will guide me, your right hand will hold me fast.

PSALM 139:7-10 NIV

MORE IDEAS ABOUT GOD'S PRESENCE

It's a crazy world and life speeds by at a blur, yet God is right in the middle of the craziness. And anywhere, at anytime, we may turn to Him, hear His voice, feel His hand, and catch the fragrance of heaven.

JONI EARECKSON TADA

God's presence is such a cleansing fire, confession and repentance are always there.

ANNE ORTLUND

What God promises is that He always, always comes. He always shows up. He always saves. He always rescues. His timing is not ours. His methods are usually unconventional. But what we can know, what we can settle in our soul, is that He is faithful to come when we call.

ANGELA THOMAS

If you want to hear God's voice clearly and you are uncertain, then remain in His presence until He changes that uncertainty. Often, much can happen during this waiting for the Lord. Sometimes, he changes pride into humility, doubt into faith and peace.

CORRIE TEN BOOM

The love of God is so vast, the power of his touch so invigorating, we could just stay in his presence for hours, soaking up his glory, basking in his blessings.

DEBRA EVANS

The Lord Jesus by His Holy Spirit is with me, and the knowledge of His presence dispels the darkness and allays any fears.

BILL BRIGHT

Whatever we have done in the past, be it good or evil, great or small, is irrelevant to our stance before God today. It is only now that we are in the presence of God.

BRENNAN MANNING

THE TIP OF THE DAY

If God is everywhere, why does He sometimes seem so far away? The answer to that question, of course, has nothing to do with God and everything to do with us. God sometimes seems far away because we have allowed ourselves to become distant from Him, not vice versa.

THE PRAYER OF THE DAY

Dear Lord, help me to feel Your presence in every situation
and every circumstance. You are with me, Lord, in times
of celebration and in times of sorrow. You are with
me when I am strong and when I am weak.
You never leave my side, even when it seems to me that
You are far away. Today and every day, God,
let me feel Your presence and accept Your love.

Amen

MY THOUGHTS ABOUT
GOD'S PRESENCE

_____

_____

_____

_____

_____

_____

_____

_____

DAY **6**

THE WISDOM OF WAITING

God wants you to live a pure life. Keep yourselves from sexual promiscuity. Learn to appreciate and give dignity to your body, not abusing it, as is so common among those who know nothing of God.

1 THESSALONIANS 4:3-5 MSG

YOU WILL LIVE WISELY AND WELL IF . . .
You wait until you're married to have sexual relations.

If you're treating your body with respect, you're doing God's will. And if you're doing God's will, you'll have an easier time building a meaningful relationship with your Father in heaven. So, if you want to know God better, you should treat your body—and thus yourself—with respect. But sometimes, that's a hard thing to do.

You live in a society that is filled to the brim with temptations, distractions, and distortions about sex. You are bombarded with images that glamorize sex outside marriage. In fact, you are subjected to daily pressures and problems that were largely unknown to earlier generations. At every corner, or so it seems, you are confronted with the message that premarital sex is a harmless activity, something that should be considered "recreational." That message is a terrible lie with tragic consequences.

When you think about it, the argument in favor of abstinence isn't a very hard case to make. First and foremost, abstinence is a part of God's plan for people who are not married. Period. But it doesn't stop there: abstinence is also the right thing to do and the smart thing to do.

God has a plan for your life, a plan that does not include sex before marriage. So do yourself a favor: take time to think carefully about the wisdom of waiting. It's your choice. Please choose wisely.

MORE FROM GOD'S WORD

*Marriage must be respected by all, and the marriage bed kept
undefiled, because God will judge immoral people and adulterers.*

HEBREWS 13:4 HCSB

*Do you not know that your body is a sanctuary of the Holy Spirit
who is in you, whom you have from God? You are not your own,
for you were bought at a price; therefore glorify God in your body.*

1 CORINTHIANS 6:19-20 HCSB

*Sow righteousness for yourselves and reap faithful love; break up
your untilled ground. It is time to seek the Lord until He comes
and sends righteousness on you like the rain.*

HOSEA 10:12 HCSB

Blessed are the pure in heart, for they shall see God.

MATTHEW 5:8 NKJV

*Are there those among you who are truly wise and understanding?
Then they should show it by living right and doing good things with
a gentleness that comes from wisdom.*

JAMES 3:13 NCV

MORE IDEAS ABOUT ABSTINENCE

The Bible has a word to describe "safe" sex. It's called marriage.

GARY SMALLEY & JOHN TRENT

But suppose we do sin. Suppose we slip and fall. Suppose we yield to temptation for a moment. What happens? We have to confess that sin.

BILLY GRAHAM

Good and evil both increase at compound interest. That is why the little decisions you and I make every day are of such infinite importance.

C. S. LEWIS

A healthy fear of God will do much to deter us from sin.

CHARLES SWINDOLL

We must recognize that when we face deeply rooted habits of sin in daily spiritual warfare, self-help is no help at all. There is only one cure, and it comes from God.

JIM CYMBALA

To a world that was spiritually dry and populated with parched lives scorched by sin, Jesus was the Living Water who would quench the thirsty soul, saving it from "bondage" and filling it with satisfaction and joy and purpose and meaning.

ANNE GRAHAM LOTZ

Identify the sin. Confess it. Turn from it. Avoid it at all costs. Live with a clean, forgiven conscience. Don't dwell on what God has forgotten!

MAX LUCADO

As a child of God, you are no longer a slave to sin.

KAY ARTHUR

THE TIP OF THE DAY
If you abstain from premarital sex, you'll be blessed and your marriage will be, too.

THE PRAYER OF THE DAY

Dear Lord, when I displease You, I do injury to myself
and to my family. Because sin distances me from You, Lord,
I will fear sin. The fear of sinning against You is a healthy
fear, Father, because it can motivate me to accomplish
Your will. Let a healthy fear of sin guide
my path, today and every day of my life.

Amen

MY THOUGHTS ABOUT ABSTINENCE

_____

_____

_____

_____

_____

_____

_____

_____

DAY 7

GOD WANTS YOU TO LIVE ABUNDANTLY

I have come that they may have life,
and that they may have it more abundantly.

JOHN 10:10 NKJV

YOU WILL LIVE WISELY AND WELL IF . . .
You open your heart and accept God's abundance.

The 10th chapter of John tells us that Christ came to earth so that our lives might be filled with abundance. But what, exactly, did Jesus mean when He promised "life . . . more abundantly"? Was He referring to material possessions, financial wealth, or personal popularity? Hardly. Jesus offers a different kind of abundance: a spiritual richness that extends beyond time and space. This everlasting abundance is available to all who seek it and claim it.

God offers us abundance and joy, but He does not force these things upon us. He promises that we "might have life" and that we "might have it more abundantly" if we accept His grace, His blessings, and His Son.

When we entrust our hearts and our days to the One who created us, we experience abundance through the grace and sacrifice of His Son, Jesus. But, when we turn our thoughts and direct our energies away from God's commandments, we squander the spiritual abundance that might otherwise be ours.

Do you sincerely seek the riches that our Savior offers to those who give themselves to Him? Then follow Him completely and without reservation. When you do, you will receive the love, the joy, and the abundance that He has promised.

MORE FROM GOD'S WORD

Until now you have asked for nothing in My name. Ask and you will receive, that your joy may be complete.

JOHN 16:24 HCSB

Come to terms with God and be at peace; in this way good will come to you.

JOB 22:21 HCSB

The master was full of praise. "Well done, my good and faithful servant. You have been faithful in handling this small amount, so now I will give you many more responsibilities. Let's celebrate together!"

MATTHEW 25:21 NLT

But this I say, He which soweth sparingly shall reap also sparingly; and he which soweth bountifully shall reap also bountifully.

2 CORINTHIANS 9:6 KJV

My cup runneth over. Surely goodness and mercy shall follow me all the days of my life: and I will dwell in the house of the LORD for ever.

PSALM 23:5-6 KJV

MORE IDEAS ABOUT
ABUNDANCE

God is the giver, and we are the receivers. And His richest gifts are bestowed not upon those who do the greatest things, but upon those who accept His abundance and His grace.

HANNAH WHITALL SMITH

If we just give God the little that we have, we can trust Him to make it go around.

GLORIA GAITHER

People, places, and things were never meant to give us life. God alone is the author of a fulfilling life.

GARY SMALLEY & JOHN TRENT

If we were given all we wanted here, our hearts would settle for this world rather than the next.

ELISABETH ELLIOT

It would be wrong to have a "poverty complex," for to think ourselves paupers is to deny either the King's riches or to deny our being His children.

CATHERINE MARSHALL

Instead of living a black-and-white existence, we'll be released into a Technicolor world of vibrancy and emotion when we more accurately reflect His nature to the world around us.

BILL HYBELS

God's riches are beyond anything we could ask or even dare to imagine! If my life gets gooey and stale, I have no excuse.

BARBARA JOHNSON

The only way you can experience abundant life is to surrender your plans to Him.

CHARLES STANLEY

THE TIP OF THE DAY

God wants you to make the most out of all the opportunities He sends your way. Billy Graham observed, "Life is a glorious opportunity." That's sound advice, so keep looking for your opportunities until you find them, and when you find them, take advantage of them sooner rather than later.

THE PRAYER OF THE DAY

Lord, as I take the next steps on my life's journey,
let me take them with You. Whatever this day may bring,
I thank You for the opportunity to live abundantly.
Let me lean upon You, Father—and trust You—
this day and forever.
Amen

MY THOUGHTS ABOUT ABUNDANCE

_____

_____

_____

_____

_____

_____

_____

_____

DAY 8

THE POWER
OF GOD'S WORD

*For the word of God is living and effective and sharper
than any two-edged sword, penetrating as far as to divide soul,
spirit, joints, and marrow; it is a judge of the ideas
and thoughts of the heart.*

HEBREWS 4:12 HCSB

YOU WILL LIVE WISELY AND WELL IF . . .
You study God's Word and live in accordance
with its teachings.

Too many Christians treat the Bible like any other book. But get this loud and clear: THE BIBLE ISN'T LIKE ANY OTHER BOOK! Period! And if you're wise, you'll give your Bible the reverence and the attention that it deserves.

Is God's Word a bright spotlight that guides your path, or is it a tiny nightlight that occasionally flickers? Is God's Word your indispensable compass for everyday living, or is it relegated to Sunday morning services? Do you read the Bible faithfully or sporadically? The answer to these questions will determine the direction of your thoughts, the direction of your day, and the direction of your life.

George Mueller observed, "The vigor of our spiritual lives will be in exact proportion to the place held by the Bible in our lives and in our thoughts." Think of it like this: the more you use your Bible, the more God will use you.

God's Word can be a roadmap to a place of righteousness and abundance. Make it your roadmap. God's wisdom can be a light to guide your steps. Claim it as your light today, tomorrow, and every day of your life—and then walk confidently in the footsteps of God's only begotten Son.

MORE FROM GOD'S WORD

All Scripture is inspired by God and is profitable for teaching, for rebuking, for correcting, for training in righteousness, so that the man of God may be complete, equipped for every good work.

2 TIMOTHY 3:16-17 HCSB

Man shall not live by bread alone, but by every word that proceeds from the mouth of God.

MATTHEW 4:4 NKJV

For I am not ashamed of the gospel, because it is God's power for salvation to everyone who believes.

ROMANS 1:16 HCSB

The one who is from God listens to God's words. This is why you don't listen, because you are not from God.

JOHN 8:47 HCSB

Heaven and earth will pass away, but My words will never pass away.

MATTHEW 24:35 HCSB

MORE IDEAS ABOUT GOD'S WORD

Either God's Word keeps you from sin, or sin keeps you from God's Word.

CORRIE TEN BOOM

God's Word is a light not only to our path but also to our thinking. Place it in your heart today, and you will never walk in darkness.

JONI EARECKSON TADA

Walking in faith brings you to the Word of God. There you will be healed, cleansed, fed, nurtured, equipped, and matured.

KAY ARTHUR

You should not believe your conscience and your feelings more than the word which the Lord who receives sinners preaches to you.

MARTIN LUTHER

If we are not continually fed with God's Word, we will starve spiritually.

STORMIE OMARTIAN

God meant that we adjust to the Gospel—not the other way around.

VANCE HAVNER

Just as you do not analyze the words of someone you love, but accept them as they are said to you, accept the Word of Scripture and ponder it in your heart.

DIETRICH BONHOEFFER

The Gospel is not so much a demand as it is an offer, an offer of new life to man by the grace of God.

E. STANLEY JONES

THE TIP OF THE DAY

The Bible is the best-selling book of all time . . . for good reason. Ruth Bell Graham, wife of evangelist Billy Graham, believed in the importance of God's Word: "The Reference Point for the Christian is the Bible. All values, judgments, and attitudes must be gauged in relationship to this Reference Point." Make certain that you're an avid reader of God's bestseller, and make sure that you keep reading it as long as you live!

THE PRAYER OF THE DAY

Lord, You've given me instructions for life here on earth
and for life eternal. I will use the Bible as my guide.
I will study it and meditate upon it as I trust You, Lord,
to speak to me through Your Holy Word.

Amen

MY THOUGHTS ABOUT
GOD'S WORD

_____

_____

_____

_____

_____

_____

_____

DAY 9

THE WORLD'S VALUES VERSUS GOD'S VALUES

Therefore, put to death whatever in you is worldly:
sexual immorality, impurity, lust, evil desire, and greed,
which is idolatry. Because of these,
God's wrath comes on the disobedient.
COLOSSIANS 3:5-6 HCSB

YOU WILL LIVE WISELY AND WELL IF . . .
You learn to resist the world's values and focus, instead,
on God's values.

God's values and the world's values are seldom the same. Although we live in the world, we must not worship it—yet at every turn, or so it seems, we are tempted to do otherwise. The 21st-century world in which we live is a noisy, distracting place, a place that offers countless temptations and dangers. The world seems to cry, "Worship me with your time, your money, your energy, your thoughts, and your life!" But if we are wise, we won't fall prey to that temptation.

If you genuinely wish to be pure, you must distance yourself, at least in part, from the temptations and distractions of modern-day society. But distancing yourself isn't easy, especially when so many societal forces are struggling to lead you far from God's path.

C. S. Lewis said, "Aim at heaven and you will get earth thrown in; aim at earth and you will get neither." That's good advice. You're likely to hit what you aim at, so aim high . . . aim at heaven. When you do, you'll be strengthening your character as you improve every aspect of your life. And God will demonstrate His approval as He showers you with more spiritual blessings than you can count.

MORE FROM GOD'S WORD

You can be sure that no immoral, impure, or greedy person will inherit the Kingdom of Christ and of God. For a greedy person is really an idolater who worships the things of this world. Don't be fooled by those who try to excuse these sins, for the terrible anger of God comes upon all those who disobey him.

EPHESIANS 5:5-6 NLT

Do not love the world or the things in the world. If you love the world, the love of the Father is not in you.

1 JOHN 2:15 NCV

For whatever is born of God overcomes the world. And this is the victory that has overcome the world—our faith.

1 JOHN 5:4 NKJV

Religion that God our Father accepts as pure and faultless is this: to look after orphans and widows in their distress and to keep oneself from being polluted by the world.

JAMES 1:27 NIV

No one should deceive himself. If anyone among you thinks he is wise in this age, he must become foolish so that he can become wise. For the wisdom of this world is foolishness with God, since it is written: He catches the wise in their craftiness.

1 CORINTHIANS 3:18-19 HCSB

MORE IDEAS ABOUT WORLDLINESS

Our fight is not against any physical enemy; it is against organizations and powers that are spiritual. We must struggle against sin all our lives, but we are assured we will win.

CORRIE TEN BOOM

The more we stuff ourselves with material pleasures, the less we seem to appreciate life.

BARBARA JOHNSON

All those who look to draw their satisfaction from the wells of the world—pleasure, popularity, position, possessions, politics, power, prestige, finances, family, friends, fame, fortune, career, children, church, clubs, sports, sex, success, recognition, reputation, religion, education, entertainment, exercise, honors, health, hobbies—will soon be thirsty again!

ANNE GRAHAM LOTZ

The only ultimate disaster that can befall us, I have come to realize, is to feel ourselves to be home on earth.

MAX LUCADO

The true Christian, though he is in revolt against the world's efforts to brainwash him, is no mere rebel for rebellion's sake. He dissents from the world because he knows that it cannot make good on its promises.

A. W. TOZER

It is impossible to please God doing things motivated by and produced by the flesh.

BILL BRIGHT

The Lord Jesus Christ is still praying for us. He wants us to be in the world but not of it.

CHARLES STANLEY

The world's sewage system threatens to contaminate the stream of Christian thought. Is the world shaping your mind, or is Christ?

BILLY GRAHAM

THE TIP OF THE DAY

The world's power to distract, detour, and destroy is formidable. Thankfully, God's power is even greater.

THE PRAYER OF THE DAY

Dear Lord, I am an imperfect human being living
in an imperfect world. Direct my path far from
the temptations and distractions of this world,
and let me follow in the footsteps
of Your Son today and forever.
Amen

MY THOUGHTS ABOUT WORLDLINESS

_____

_____

_____

_____

_____

_____

_____

_____

DAY **10**

GOD'S LOVE = REAL LOVE

This is what real love is: It is not our love for God;
it is God's love for us in sending his Son
to be the way to take away our sins.

1 JOHN 4:10 NCV

YOU WILL LIVE WISELY AND WELL IF . . .
You recognize the transforming power of God's love.

God is love. It's a sweeping statement, a profoundly important description of what God is and how God works. God's love is perfect. When we open our hearts to His perfect love, we are touched by the Creator's hand, and we are transformed.

Barbara Johnson observed, "We cannot protect ourselves from trouble, but we can dance through the puddles of life with a rainbow smile, twirling the only umbrella we need—the umbrella of God's love."

As the English mystical writer Juliana of Norwich noted, "We are so preciously loved by God that we cannot even comprehend it. No created being can ever know how much and how sweetly and tenderly God loves them."

So today, even if you can only carve out a few quiet moments, offer sincere prayers of thanksgiving to your Father. Thank Him for His blessings and His love.

MORE FROM GOD'S WORD

Unfailing love surrounds those who trust the LORD.

PSALM 32:10 NLT

For the LORD your God has arrived to live among you. He is a mighty savior. He will rejoice over you with great gladness. With his love, he will calm all your fears. He will exult over you by singing a happy song.

ZEPHANIAH 3:17 NLT

For God loved the world in this way: He gave His only Son, so that everyone who believes in Him will not perish but have eternal life.

JOHN 3:16 HCSB

The unfailing love of the Lord never ends!

LAMENTATIONS 3:22 NLT

But God demonstrates his own love for us in this: While we were still sinners, Christ died for us.

ROMANS 5:8 NIV

MORE IDEAS ABOUT GOD'S LOVE

Believing that you are loved will set you free to be who God created you to be. So rest in His love and just be yourself.

LISA WHELCHEL

The fact is, God no longer deals with us in judgment but in mercy. If people got what they deserved, this old planet would have ripped apart at the seams centuries ago. Praise God that because of His great love "we are not consumed, for his compassions never fail" (Lam. 3:22).

JONI EARECKSON TADA

Being loved by Him whose opinion matters most gives us the security to risk loving, too—even loving ourselves.

GLORIA GAITHER

There is no pit so deep that God's love is not deeper still.

CORRIE TEN BOOM

Even when we cannot see the why and wherefore of God's dealings, we know that there is love in and behind them, so we can rejoice always.

J. I. PACKER

God proved his love on the cross. When Christ hung, and bled, and died, it was God saying to the world—I love you.

BILLY GRAHAM

God is my heavenly Father. He loves me with an everlasting love. The proof of that is the Cross.

ELISABETH ELLIOT

God is the sunshine that warms us, the rain that melts the frost and waters the young plants. The presence of God is a climate of strong and bracing love, always there.

JOAN ARNOLD

THE TIP OF THE DAY

God's love is your greatest security blanket. Kay Arthur advises, "Snuggle in God's arms. When you are hurting, when you feel lonely or left out, let Him cradle you, comfort you, reassure you of His all-sufficient power and love." Enough said.

THE PRAYER OF THE DAY

Lord, Your love is infinite and eternal. Although I cannot
fully understand the depths of Your love, I can praise it,
return it, and share it . . . today and every day.

Amen

MY THOUGHTS ABOUT GOD'S LOVE

_____

_____

_____

_____

_____

_____

_____

_____

DAY 11

YOU CAN OVERCOME YOUR MISTAKES

*The Lord says, "Forget what happened before, and do not think
about the past. Look at the new thing I am going to do.
It is already happening. Don't you see it?
I will make a road in the desert and rivers in the dry land."*

ISAIAH 43:18-19 NCV

YOU WILL LIVE WISELY AND WELL IF . . .
You recognize that mistakes are never final
and that you can be forgiven.

We are imperfect beings living in an imperfect world; mistakes are simply part of the price we pay for being here. Yet, even though mistakes are an inevitable part of life's journey, repeated mistakes should not be. When we commit the inevitable blunders of life, we must correct them, learn from them, and pray for the wisdom to avoid those same mistakes in the future. If we are successful, our missteps become lessons, and our lives become adventures in growth.

Mistakes are the price we pay for being human; repeated mistakes are the price we pay for being stubborn. But, if we are wise enough to learn from our experiences, we continue to mature throughout every stage of life. And that's precisely what God intends for us to do.

MORE FROM GOD'S WORD

If you hide your sins, you will not succeed. If you confess and reject them, you will receive mercy.

PROVERBS 28:13 NCV

If you listen to constructive criticism, you will be at home among the wise.

PROVERBS 15:31 NLT

I will instruct you and teach you in the way you should go; I will counsel you and watch over you.

PSALM 32:8 NIV

God is our refuge and strength, a very present help in trouble.

PSALM 46:1 NKJV

Therefore, if anyone is in Christ, he is a new creation; the old has gone, the new has come!

2 CORINTHIANS 5:17 NIV

MORE IDEAS ABOUT MISTAKES

No matter how badly we have failed, we can always get up and begin again. Our God is the God of new beginnings.

WARREN WIERSBE

God is able to take mistakes, when they are committed to Him, and make of them something for our good and for His glory.

RUTH BELL GRAHAM

There is nothing wrong with asking God's direction. But it is wrong to go our own way, then expect Him to bail us out.

LARRY BURKETT

Mistakes offer the possibility for redemption and a new start in God's kingdom. No matter what you're guilty of, God can restore your innocence.

BARBARA JOHNSON

We become a failure when we allow mistakes to take away our ability to learn, give, grow, and try again.

SUSAN LENZKES

Lord, when we are wrong, make us willing to change; and when we are right, make us easy to live with.

PETER MARSHALL

If you're willing to repair your life, God is willing to help. If you're not willing to repair your life, God is willing to wait.

MARIE T. FREEMAN

Truth will sooner come out of error than from confusion.

FRANCIS BACON

THE TIP OF THE DAY

Failure isn't permanent . . . unless you fail to get back up. So pick yourself up, dust yourself off, and trust God. He will make it right. Warren Wiersbe had this advice: "No matter how badly we have failed, we can always get up and begin again. Our God is the God of new beginnings." And don't forget: the best time to begin again is now.

THE PRAYER OF THE DAY

Dear Lord, sometimes I make mistakes.
When I do, help me learn something,
help me forgive myself, and help me become
a smarter person today than I was yesterday.
Amen

MY THOUGHTS ABOUT MISTAKES

_____

_____

_____

_____

_____

_____

_____

DAY 12

SEEKING GOD'S WILL

And this world is fading away, along with everything it craves.
But if you do the will of God, you will live forever.
1 JOHN 2:17 NLT

YOU WILL LIVE WISELY AND WELL IF . . .
You seek God's will and follow it.

God has a plan for our world and our lives. God does not do things by accident; He is willful and intentional. Unfortunately for us, we simply cannot always understand the willful heart of God. Why? Because we are mortal beings with limited understanding. Thus, we can never fully comprehend the will of God. But as believers in a benevolent Heavenly Father, we must always trust the will of God.

Before His crucifixion, Jesus went to the Mount of Olives and poured out His heart to God (Luke 22). Jesus knew of the agony that He was destined to endure, but He also knew that God's will must be done. We, like our Savior, face trials that bring fear and trembling to the very depths of our souls, but like Christ, we, too, must ultimately seek God's will, not our own.

As this day unfolds, seek God's will and obey His Word. When you entrust your life to Him completely and without reservation, He will give you the strength to overcome any temptation, the courage to face any trial, and the wisdom to live in His righteousness and in His peace.

More from God's Word

He is the Lord. He will do what He thinks is good.

1 Samuel 3:18 HCSB

Teach me your ways, O Lord, that I may live according to your truth! Grant me purity of heart, that I may honor you.

Psalm 86:11 NLT

Commit your activities to the Lord and your plans will be achieved.

Proverbs 16:3 HCSB

My Father! If it is possible, let this cup pass from Me. Yet not as I will, but as You will.

Matthew 26:39 HCSB

Don't copy the behavior and customs of this world, but let God transform you into a new person by changing the way you think. Then you will know what God wants you to do, and you will know how good and pleasing and perfect his will really is.

Romans 12:2 NLT

MORE IDEAS ABOUT GOD'S WILL

Make God's will the focus of your life day by day. If you seek to please Him and Him alone, you'll find yourself satisfied with life.

KAY ARTHUR

Our sense of joy, satisfaction, and fulfillment in life increases, no matter what the circumstances, if we are in the center of God's will.

BILLY GRAHAM

The will of God is never exactly what you expect it to be. It may seem to be much worse, but in the end it's going to be a lot better and a lot bigger.

ELISABETH ELLIOT

Jesus yielded Himself to the Father's will. He was a model of "reverent submission." Jesus lived a life of prayer, faith, and obedience.

SHIRLEY DOBSON

To walk out of His will is to walk into nowhere.

C. S. LEWIS

Absolute submission is not enough; we should go on to joyful acquiescence to the will of God.

C. H. SPURGEON

"If the Lord will" is not just a statement on a believer's lips; it is the constant attitude of his heart.

WARREN WIERSBE

God is God. He knows what he is doing. When you can't trace his hand, trust his heart.

MAX LUCADO

THE TIP OF THE DAY

One of the most important lessons that you can ever learn is to trust God for everything—not some things, not most things . . . everything!

THE PRAYER OF THE DAY

Dear Lord, You are the Creator of the universe,
and I know that Your plan for my life is grander than
I can imagine. Let Your purposes be my purposes.
Let Your will be my will. When I am confused, give me
clarity. When I am worried, give me strength. Let me be
Your faithful servant, Lord, always seeking Your guidance
and Your will for my life. Let me live this day and every day
according to Your commandments and with the assurance
of Your promises, in Jesus' name I pray.

Amen

MY THOUGHTS ABOUT
GOD'S WILL

_____

_____

_____

_____

_____

_____

_____

DAY 13

ASK GOD

So I say to you, keep asking, and it will be given to you.
Keep searching, and you will find.
Keep knocking, and the door will be opened to you.
LUKE 11:9 HCSB

YOU WILL LIVE WISELY AND WELL IF . . .
You learn to ask God for what you need.

How often do you ask God for His help and His wisdom? Occasionally? Intermittently? Whenever you experience a crisis? Hopefully not. Hopefully, you've acquired the habit of asking for God's assistance early and often. And hopefully, you have learned to seek His guidance in every aspect of your life.

The Bible promises that God will guide you if you let Him. Your job is to let Him. But sometimes, you will be tempted to do otherwise. Sometimes, you'll be tempted to go along with the crowd; other times, you'll be tempted to do things your way, not God's way. When you feel those temptations, resist them.

God has promised that when you ask for His help, He will not withhold it. So ask. Ask Him to meet the needs of your day. Ask Him to lead you, to protect you, and to correct you. And trust the answers He gives.

God stands at the door and waits. When you knock, He opens. When you ask, He answers. Your task, of course, is to seek His guidance prayerfully, confidently, and often.

MORE FROM GOD'S WORD

You did not choose me, but I chose you and appointed you to go and bear fruit—fruit that will last. Then the Father will give you whatever you ask in my name.

JOHN 15:16 NIV

Do not worry about anything, but pray and ask God for everything you need, always giving thanks.

PHILIPPIANS 4:6 NCV

You do not have, because you do not ask God.

JAMES 4:2 NIV

You fathers—if your children ask for a fish, do you give them a snake instead? Or if they ask for an egg, do you give them a scorpion? Of course not! If you sinful people know how to give good gifts to your children, how much more will your heavenly Father give the Holy Spirit to those who ask him.

LUKE 11:11-13 NLT

Ask in my name, according to my will, and he'll most certainly give it to you. Your joy will be a river overflowing its banks!

JOHN 16:24 MSG

MORE IDEAS ABOUT ASKING GOD

By asking in Jesus' name, we're making a request not only in His authority, but also for His interests and His benefit.

SHIRLEY DOBSON

God will help us become the people we are meant to be, if only we will ask Him.

HANNAH WHITALL SMITH

When trials come your way—as inevitably they will—do not run away. Run to your God and Father.

KAY ARTHUR

All we have to do is to acknowledge our need, move from self-sufficiency to dependence, and ask God to become our hiding place.

BILL HYBELS

Don't be afraid to ask your heavenly Father for anything you need. Indeed, nothing is too small for God's attention or too great for his power.

DENNIS SWANBERG

When you ask God to do something, don't ask timidly; put your whole heart into it.

MARIE T. FREEMAN

When will we realize that we're not troubling God with our questions and concerns? His heart is open to hear us—his touch nearer than our next thought—as if no one in the world existed but us. Our very personal God wants to hear from us personally.

GIGI GRAHAM TCHIVIDJIAN

Some people think God does not like to be troubled with our constant asking. But, the way to trouble God is not to come at all.

D. L. MOODY

THE TIP OF THE DAY

Today, think of a specific need that is weighing heavily on your heart. Then, spend a few quiet moments asking God for His guidance and for His help.

THE PRAYER OF THE DAY

Dear Lord, today I will ask You for the things I need.
In every circumstance, in every season of life,
I will come to You in prayer. You know the desires
of my heart, Lord; grant them, I ask. Yet not my will,
Father, but Your will be done.
Amen

MY THOUGHTS ABOUT
ASKING GOD

_____

_____

_____

_____

_____

_____

_____

DAY 14

TRUE DISCIPLESHIP

Then He said to them all, "If anyone wants to come with Me, he must deny himself, take up his cross daily, and follow Me."

LUKE 9:23 HCSB

YOU WILL LIVE WISELY AND WELL IF . . .
You decide to be Christ's disciple.

When Jesus addressed His disciples, He warned that each one must, "take up his cross and follow me." The disciples must have known exactly what the Master meant. In Jesus' day, prisoners were forced to carry their own crosses to the location where they would be put to death. Thus, Christ's message was clear: in order to follow Him, Christ's disciples must deny themselves and, instead, trust Him completely. Nothing has changed since then. The cost of discipleship is high, but it's worth it.

If we are to be disciples of Christ, we must trust Him and place Him at the very center of our beings. Jesus never comes "next." He is always first. The paradox, of course, is that only by sacrificing ourselves to Him do we gain salvation for ourselves.

Do you seek to be a worthy disciple of Christ? And do you genuinely desire to be a woman of purity and wisdom? Then pick up His cross today and every day that you live. When you do, He will bless you now and forever.

MORE FROM GOD'S WORD

Whoever is not willing to carry the cross and follow me is not worthy of me. Those who try to hold on to their lives will give up true life. Those who give up their lives for me will hold on to true life.

MATTHEW 10:38-39 NCV

I've laid down a pattern for you. What I've done, you do.

JOHN 13:15 MSG

No one can serve two masters. Either he will hate the one and love the other, or he will be devoted to the one and despise the other.

MATTHEW 6:24 NIV

But thanks be to God! He gives us the victory through our Lord Jesus Christ. Therefore, my dear brothers, stand firm. Let nothing move you. Always give yourselves fully to the work of the Lord, because you know that your labor in the Lord is not in vain.

1 CORINTHIANS 15:57-58 NIV

Work hard, but not just to please your masters when they are watching. As slaves of Christ, do the will of God with all your heart. Work with enthusiasm, as though you were working for the Lord rather than for people.

EPHESIANS 6:6-7 NLT

MORE IDEAS ABOUT DISCIPLESHIP

We must appropriate the tender mercy of God every day after conversion or problems quickly develop. We need his grace daily in order to live a righteous life.

JIM CYMBALA

Make a plan now to keep a daily appointment with God. The enemy is going to tell you to set it aside, but you must carve out the time. If you're too busy to meet with the Lord, friend, then you are simply too busy.

CHARLES SWINDOLL

It is necessary to eat every day to maintain strength and energy. When we don't, our bodies weaken. The same is true with our spirits. To maintain spiritual strength, we must feed our spirits every day with the Word of God, our spiritual food.

CYNTHIA HEALD

Our devotion to God is strengthened when we offer Him a fresh commitment each day.

ELIZABETH GEORGE

If we really believe not only that God exists but also that God is actively present in our lives—healing, teaching, and guiding—we need to set aside a time and space to give God our undivided attention.

HENRI NOUWEN

God is a place of safety you can run to, but it helps if you are running to Him on a daily basis so that you are in familiar territory.

STORMIE OMARTIAN

THE TIP OF THE DAY

When you decide to walk in the footsteps of the Master, that means that you're agreeing to be a disciple seven days a week, not just on Sunday. Remember the words of Vance Havner: "We must live in all kinds of days, both high days and low days, in simple dependence upon Christ as the branch on the vine. This is the supreme experience."

THE PRAYER OF THE DAY

Dear Jesus, because I am Your disciple, I will trust You,
I will obey Your teachings, and I will share
Your Good News. You have given me life abundant
and life eternal, and I will follow You today and forever.

Amen

MY THOUGHTS ABOUT DISCIPLESHIP

_____

_____

_____

_____

_____

_____

_____

DAY 15

GAINING SPIRITUAL MATURITY

When I was a child, I spoke and thought and reasoned
as a child does. But when I grew up, I put away childish things.
1 CORINTHIANS 13:11 NLT

YOU WILL LIVE WISELY AND WELL IF . . .
You decide to keep growing spiritually.

When will you be a "fully-grown" Christian woman? Hopefully never—or at least not until you arrive in heaven! As a believer living here on planet earth, you're never "fully grown"; you always have the potential to keep growing.

Many of life's most important lessons are painful to learn, but spiritual growth need not take place only in times of pain and hardship. Whatever your circumstances, God is always standing at the door; whenever you are ready to reach out to Him, He will answer.

In those quiet moments when you open your heart to God, the One who made you keeps remaking you. He gives you direction, perspective, wisdom, and courage. And, the appropriate moment to accept those spiritual gifts is always the present one.

Would you like a time-tested formula for spiritual growth? Here it is: keep studying God's Word, keep obeying His commandments, keep praying (and listening for answers), and seek to live in the center of God's will. When you do, you will never be a "stagnant" believer. You will, instead, be a growing Christian . . . and that's precisely the kind of Christian God wants you to be.

MORE FROM GOD'S WORD

Consider it pure joy, my brothers, whenever you face trials of many kinds, because you know that the testing of your faith develops perseverance. Perseverance must finish its work so that you may be mature and complete, not lacking anything.

JAMES 1:2-4 NIV

But grow in the grace and knowledge of our Lord and Savior Jesus Christ.

2 PETER 3:18 NIV

Therefore let us leave the elementary teachings about Christ and go on to maturity . . . .

HEBREWS 6:1 NIV

This is why I remind you to keep using the gift God gave you when I laid my hands on you. Now let it grow, as a small flame grows into a fire.

2 TIMOTHY 1:6 NCV

Know the love of Christ which surpasses knowledge, that you may be filled up to all the fullness of God.

EPHESIANS 3:19 NASB

MORE IDEAS ABOUT
SPIRITUAL MATURITY

Grow, dear friends, but grow, I beg you, in God's way, which is the only true way.

HANNAH WHITALL SMITH

If all struggles and sufferings were eliminated, the spirit would no more reach maturity than would the child.

ELISABETH ELLIOT

Maturity in Christ is about consistent pursuit in spite of the attacks and setbacks. It is about remaining in the arms of God. Abiding and staying, even in my weakness, even in my failure.

ANGELA THOMAS

We set our eyes on the finish line, forgetting the past, and straining toward the mark of spiritual maturity and fruitfulness.

VONETTE BRIGHT

Growing up in Christ is surely the most difficult, courageous, exhilarating, and eternally important work any of us will ever do.

SUSAN LENZKES

You are either becoming more like Christ every day or you're becoming less like Him. There is no neutral position in the Lord.

STORMIE OMARTIAN

There is nothing more important than understanding God's truth and being changed by it, so why are we so casual about accepting the popular theology of the moment without checking it out for ourselves? God has given us a mind so that we can learn and grow. As his people, we have a great responsibility and wonderful privilege of growing in our understanding of him.

SHEILA WALSH

THE TIP OF THE DAY

If you're going through difficult times, consider it an opportunity for spiritual growth. Elisabeth Elliot correctly observed, "God's curriculum will always include lessons we wish we could skip. With an intimate understanding of our deepest needs and individual capacities, He chooses our curriculum." So ask yourself this question: "What is God trying to teach me today?"

THE PRAYER OF THE DAY
Lord, help me to keep growing spiritually
and emotionally. Let me live according to Your Word,
and let me grow in my faith every day that I live.
Amen

MY THOUGHTS ABOUT
SPIRITUAL MATURITY

_____

_____

_____

_____

_____

_____

_____

_____

DAY 16

PRAY EARLY
AND OFTEN

Rejoice always! Pray constantly.
Give thanks in everything, for this is God's will
for you in Christ Jesus.

1 Thessalonians 5:16-18 HCSB

YOU WILL LIVE WISELY AND WELL IF . . .
You recognize the power and the importance of prayer.

I s prayer an integral part of your daily life, or is it a hit-or-miss habit? Do you "pray without ceasing," or is your prayer life an afterthought? Do you regularly pray in the quiet moments of the early morning, or do you bow your head only when others are watching?

As Christians, we are instructed to pray often. But it is important to note that genuine prayer requires much more than bending our knees and closing our eyes. Heartfelt prayer is an attitude of the heart.

If your prayers have become more a matter of habit than a matter of passion, you're robbing yourself of a deeper relationship with God. And how can you rectify this situation? By praying more frequently and more fervently. When you do, God will shower you with His blessings, His grace, and His love.

The quality of your spiritual life will be in direct proportion to the quality of your prayer life: the more you pray, the closer you will feel to God. So today, instead of turning things over in your mind, turn them over to God in prayer. Instead of worrying about your next decision, ask God to lead the way. Don't limit your prayers to the dinner table or the bedside table. Pray constantly about things great and small. God is always listening; it's up to you to do the rest.

MORE FROM GOD'S WORD

I want men everywhere to lift up holy hands in prayer, without anger or disputing.

1 TIMOTHY 2:8 NIV

If my people who are called by my name, will humble themselves and pray and seek my face and turn from their wicked ways, then will I hear from heaven and will forgive their sin and will heal their land.

2 CHRONICLES 7:14 NIV

The intense prayer of the righteous is very powerful.

JAMES 5:16 HCSB

Rejoice in hope; be patient in affliction; be persistent in prayer.

ROMANS 12:12 HCSB

Let the words of my mouth and the meditation of my heart be acceptable in Your sight, O Lord, my strength and my Redeemer.

PSALM 19:14 NKJV

MORE IDEAS ABOUT PRAYER

God is always listening.

STORMIE OMARTIAN

Next to the wonder of seeing my Savior will be, I think, the wonder that I made so little use of the power of prayer.

D. L. MOODY

As we join together in prayer, we draw on God's enabling might in a way that multiplies our own efforts many times over.

SHIRLEY DOBSON

The center of power is not to be found in summit meetings or in peace conferences. It is not in Peking or Washington or the United Nations, but rather where a child of God prays in the power of the Spirit for God's will to be done in her life, in her home, and in the world around her.

RUTH BELL GRAHAM

We must leave it to God to answer our prayers in His own wisest way. Sometimes, we are so impatient and think that God does not answer. God always answers! He never fails! Be still. Abide in Him.

MRS. CHARLES E. COWMAN

When you ask God to do something, don't ask timidly; put your whole heart into it.

MARIE T. FREEMAN

God delights in the prayers of His children—prayers that express our love for Him, prayers that share our deepest burdens with Him.

BILLY GRAHAM

Are you weak? Weary? Confused? Troubled? Pressured? How is your relationship with God? Is it held in its place of priority? I believe the greater the pressure, the greater your need for time alone with Him.

KAY ARTHUR

THE TIP OF THE DAY

Prayer strengthens your relationship with God . . . so pray. Beth Moore writes, "Prayer keeps us in constant communion with God, which is the goal of our entire believing lives." It's up to you to live—and pray— accordingly.

THE PRAYER OF THE DAY

Dear Lord, Your Holy Word commands me to pray
without ceasing. Let me take everything to You in prayer.
When I am discouraged, You can give me hope. When I am
bitter, You can heal my heart. When I am angry,
You can help me forgive. In all things great and small,
at all times, whether happy or sad, let me seek Your wisdom
and Your grace . . . in prayer.

Amen

MY THOUGHTS ABOUT PRAYER

_____

_____

_____

_____

_____

_____

_____

_____

DAY 17

GOD WANTS YOU TO SERVE OTHERS

So prepare your minds for service and have self-control.
All your hope should be for the gift of grace that will be yours
when Jesus Christ is shown to you.

1 PETER 1:13 NCV

YOU WILL LIVE WISELY AND WELL IF . . .
You recognize the importance of serving others.

We live in a world that glorifies power, prestige, appearances, fame, and money. But the words of Jesus teach us that the most esteemed men and women in this world are not the self-congratulatory leaders of society but are instead the humblest of servants.

Are you willing to become a humble servant for Christ? Are you willing to pitch in and make the world a better place, or are you determined to keep all your blessings to yourself? The answer to these questions will determine the quantity and the quality of the service you render to God and to His children.

Today, you may feel the temptation to take more than you give. You may be tempted to withhold your generosity. Or you may be tempted to build yourself up in the eyes of your friends. Resist those temptations. Instead, serve your friends quietly and without fanfare. Find a need and fill it . . . humbly. Lend a helping hand . . . anonymously. Share a word of kindness . . . with quiet sincerity. As you go about your daily activities, remember that the Savior of all humanity made Himself a servant, and we, as His followers, must do no less.

MORE FROM GOD'S WORD

There are different kinds of gifts, but they are all from the same Spirit. There are different ways to serve but the same Lord to serve.

1 CORINTHIANS 12:4–5 NCV

Therefore, since we receive a kingdom which cannot be shaken, let us show gratitude, by which we may offer to God an acceptable service with reverence and awe . . . .

HEBREWS 12:28 NASB

If they serve Him obediently, they will end their days in prosperity and their years in happiness.

JOB 36:11 HCSB

Those of us who are strong and able in the faith need to step in and lend a hand to those who falter, and not just do what is most convenient for us. Strength is for service, not status. Each one of us needs to look after the good of the people around us, asking ourselves, "How can I help?"

ROMANS 15:1-2 MSG

The greatest among you must be a servant. But those who exalt themselves will be humbled, and those who humble themselves will be exalted.

MATTHEW 23:11-12 NLT

MORE IDEAS ABOUT SERVICE

Jesus never asks us to give Him what we don't have. But He does demand that we give Him all we do have if we want to be a part of what He wishes to do in the lives of those around us!

ANNE GRAHAM LOTZ

God wants us to serve Him with a willing spirit, one that would choose no other way.

BETH MOORE

No life can surpass that of a man who quietly continues to serve God in the place where providence has placed him.

C. H. SPURGEON

A Christian is a perfectly free lord of all, subject to none. A Christian is a perfectly dutiful servant of all, subject to all.

MARTIN LUTHER

If doing a good act in public will excite others to do more good, then "Let your Light shine to all." Miss no opportunity to do good.

JOHN WESLEY

You can judge how far you have risen in the scale of life by asking one question: How wisely and how deeply do I care? To be Christianized is to be sensitized. Christians are people who care.

E. STANLEY JONES

Doing something positive toward another person is a practical approach to feeling good about yourself.

BARBARA JOHNSON

We can never untangle all the woes in other people's lives. We can't produce miracles overnight. But we can bring a cup of cool water to a thirsty soul or a scoop of laughter to a lonely heart.

BARBARA JOHNSON

THE TIP OF THE DAY

You don't need to travel around the world to serve. Someone very near you may need a helping hand or a kind word, so keep your eyes open, and look for people who need your help, whether at home, at church, or at school.

THE PRAYER OF THE DAY

Dear Lord, give me a servant's heart. When Jesus humbled
Himself and became a servant, He also became an example
for His followers. Make me a faithful steward of my gifts,
and let me share with those in need.

Amen

MY THOUGHTS ABOUT
SERVICE

_____

_____

_____

_____

_____

_____

_____

_____

DAY 18

FINDING FRIENDS WHO MAKE YOU STRONGER

I give thanks to my God for every remembrance of you.

Philippians 1:3 HCSB

YOU WILL LIVE WISELY AND WELL IF . . .
You find—and keep—friends who make you stronger.

D o you associate with people who make you a better Christian, or are you spending time with folks who encourage you to stray from your faith? The answer to this question will have a surprising impact on the condition of your spiritual health. Why? Because peer pressure is very real and very powerful. That's why one of the best ways to ensure that you follow Christ is to find fellow believers who are willing to follow Him with you.

Our world is filled with pressures: some good, some bad. The pressures that we feel to follow God's will and obey His commandments are positive pressures. God places them in our hearts so that we might act in accordance with His will. But we also face different pressures, ones that are definitely not from God. When we feel pressured to do things—or even to think thoughts—that lead us away from Him, we must beware.

Many elements of society seek to mold us into more worldly beings; God, on the other hand, seeks to mold us into new beings, new creations through Christ, beings that are most certainly not conformed to this world. If we are to please God, we must resist the pressures that society seeks to impose upon us, and we must conform ourselves, instead, to His will, to His path, and to His Son.

MORE FROM GOD'S WORD

As iron sharpens iron, a friend sharpens a friend.

PROVERBS 27:17 NLT

Beloved, if God so loved us, we also ought to love one another.

1 JOHN 4:11 NKJV

This is my command: Love one another the way I loved you. This is the very best way to love. Put your life on the line for your friends.

JOHN 15:12-13 MSG

He who walks with wise men will be wise, but the companion of fools will be destroyed.

PROVERBS 13:20 NKJV

Blessed is the man who walks not in the counsel of the ungodly, nor stands in the path of sinners, nor sits in the seat of the scornful; but his delight is in the law of the Lord, and in His law he meditates day and night.

PSALM 1:1-2 NKJV

MORE IDEAS ABOUT FRIENDS

Trust is the soil in which the flower of friendship grows.

MARIE T. FREEMAN

In friendship, God opens your eyes to the glories of Himself.

JONI EARECKSON TADA

Friendships are living organisms at work. They continue to unfold, change, and emerge.

BARBARA JOHNSON

The glory of friendship is not the outstretched hand, or the kindly smile, or the joy of companionship. It is the spiritual inspiration that comes to one when he discovers that someone else believes in him and is willing to trust him with his friendship.

CORRIE TEN BOOM

Though I know intellectually how vulnerable I am to pride and power, I am the last one to know when I succumb to their seduction. That's why spiritual Lone Rangers are so dangerous—and why we must depend on trusted brothers and sisters who love us enough to tell us the truth.

CHUCK COLSON

Don't bypass the potential for meaningful friendships just because of differences. Explore them. Embrace them. Love them.

LUCI SWINDOLL

I have found that the closer I am to the godly people around me, the easier it is for me to live a righteous life because they hold me accountable.

JOHN MACARTHUR

Yes, the Spirit was sent to be our Counselor. Yes, Jesus speaks to us personally. But often he works through another human being.

JOHN ELDREDGE

THE TIP OF THE DAY

If you choose friends who behave themselves . . . you'll be far more likely to behave yourself, too. And when you do, you'll feel better about your friends and yourself.

THE PRAYER OF THE DAY

Dear Lord, let my friendships honor You.
Keep me mindful that I am Your servant in every aspect
of my life. Let me be a worthy servant, Lord,
and a worthy friend. And, may the love of Jesus shine
in me and through me today and forever.

Amen

MY THOUGHTS ABOUT FRIENDS

_____

_____

_____

_____

_____

_____

_____

_____

DAY 19

YOU ARE THE LIGHT . . . DON'T HIDE IT

You are the light of the world. A city set on a hill cannot be hidden;
nor does anyone light a lamp and put it under a basket,
but on the lampstand, and it gives light to all who are in the house.
Let your light shine before men in such a way that they may see
your good works, and glorify your Father who is in heaven.

MATTHEW 5:14–16 NASB

YOU WILL LIVE WISELY AND WELL IF . . .
You understand the importance of sharing your testimony.

L et's face it: those of us who are Christians should be willing to talk about the things that Christ has done for us. Our personal testimonies are vitally important, but sometimes, because of shyness or insecurities, we're afraid to share our experiences. And that's unfortunate.

In his second letter to Timothy, Paul shares a message to believers of every generation when he writes, "God has not given us a spirit of timidity" (1:7). Paul's meaning is crystal clear: When sharing our testimonies, we must be courageous, forthright, and unashamed.

We live in a world that desperately needs the healing message of Christ Jesus. Every believer, each in his or her own way, bears responsibility for sharing the Good News of our Savior. And it is important to remember that we bear testimony through both words and actions.

Billy Graham observed, "Our faith grows by expression. If we want to keep our faith, we must share it." If you are a follower of Christ, the time to express your belief in Him is now. You know how Jesus has touched your heart; help Him do the same for others.

MORE FROM GOD'S WORD

But the following night the Lord stood by him and said, "Be of good cheer, Paul; for as you have testified for Me."

ACTS 23:11 NKJV

But respect Christ as the holy Lord in your hearts. Always be ready to answer everyone who asks you to explain about the hope you have.

1 PETER 3:15 NCV

This and this only has been my appointed work: getting this news to those who have never heard of God, and explaining how it works by simple faith and plain truth.

1 TIMOTHY 2:7 MSG

And I assure you of this: If anyone acknowledges me publicly here on earth, I, the Son of Man, will openly acknowledge that person in the presence of God's angels. But if anyone denies me here on earth, I will deny that person before God's angels.

LUKE 12:8-9 NLT

Whatever I tell you in the dark, speak in the light; and what you hear in the ear, preach on the housetops.

MATTHEW 10:27 NKJV

MORE IDEAS ABOUT TESTIMONY

There are many timid souls whom we jostle morning and evening as we pass them by; but if only the kind word were spoken they might become fully persuaded.

FANNY CROSBY

We are the earthen vessels, the jars of clay, that bring the life and love of Christ to one another.

SHEILA WALSH

It's a joy to share my faith. I've found something so special that I want others to share in it. When something is that close to your heart, share it.

MICHAEL CHANG

Theology is an interesting school of thought. The Bible is beautiful literature. Sitting in quiet sanctuary, bathed in the amber light from stained-glass windows, having our jangled nerves soothed by the chords from an organ—all that is inspiring. But to tell you the truth, when we leave the classroom, close the church door, and walk out into the real world, it is the indisputable proof of changed lives that makes us believers.

GLORIA GAITHER

There is nothing more appealing or convincing to a watching world than to hear the testimony of someone who has just been with Jesus.

HENRY BLACKABY

You cannot keep silent once you have experienced salvation of Jesus Christ.

WARREN WIERSBE

We need to talk to God about people, then talk to people about God.

DIETER ZANDER

THE TIP OF THE DAY

Your story is important: D. L. Moody, the famed evangelist from Chicago, said, "Remember, a small light will do a great deal when it is in a very dark place. Put one little tallow candle in the middle of a large hall, and it will give a great deal of light." Make certain that your candle is always lit. Give your testimony, and trust God to do the rest.

THE PRAYER OF THE DAY

Dear Lord, let me share the Good News of Jesus with
a world that so desperately needs His peace
and His salvation. Today, let me share the message
of Your Son through my words and by my deeds.

Amen

MY THOUGHTS ABOUT
TESTIMONY

_____

_____

_____

_____

_____

_____

_____

_____

DAY 20

MAKING THE CHOICE TO WAIT UNTIL YOU'RE MARRIED

The thing you should want most is God's kingdom
and doing what God wants. Then all these other things
you need will be given to you.

MATTHEW 6:33 NCV

YOU WILL LIVE WISELY AND WELL IF . . .
You make wise choices especially when
you're making BIG choices.

Life is a series of choices. From the instant we wake in the morning until the moment we nod off to sleep at night, we make countless decisions: decisions about the things we do, decisions about the words we speak, and decisions about the thoughts we choose to think. Simply put, the quality of those decisions determines the quality of our lives. And, one of the most important choices you have to make concerns sex and marriage.

The decision to have sex before you're married—or the decision to abstain from it—is a choice that will most certainly impact the rest of your life. That decision will play an important role in the way you see yourself, and it will play an important role in the way you view relationships with members of the opposite sex. And of course, there's always the chance that your decision to have sex might result in an unexpected "surprise."

Face it: there's a lot riding on the decision to abstain from sex. And because it's an important decision, you should think about it—and pray about it—before you make a decision that might just change the direction of your life.

Perhaps you have friends who boast about sex. If so, it may seem to you that "everybody is doing it." But they're not. In fact, millions of young adults know that premarital sex is just plain wrong. And you must understand it, too.

If you're involved with people who try to convince you that it's okay to have sex before marriage, you're hanging out with the wrong people. So do yourself a favor: find friends who know that everybody isn't doing it . . . because they aren't!

MORE FROM GOD'S WORD

So I strive always to keep my conscience clear before God and man.

ACTS 24:16 NIV

If you don't know what you're doing, pray to the Father. He loves to help. You'll get his help, and won't be condescended to when you ask for it. Ask boldly, believingly, without a second thought. People who "worry their prayers" are like wind-whipped waves. Don't think you're going to get anything from the Master that way, adrift at sea, keeping all your options open.

JAMES 1:5-8 MSG

Above all and before all, do this: Get Wisdom! Write this at the top of your list: Get Understanding!

PROVERBS 4:7 MSG

The wise people will shine like the brightness of the sky. Those who teach others to live right will shine like stars forever and ever.

DANIEL 12:3 NCV

MORE IDEAS ABOUT CHOICES

Every day, I find countless opportunities to decide whether I will obey God and demonstrate my love for Him or try to please myself or the world system. God is waiting for my choices.

BILL BRIGHT

Every time you make a choice, you are turning the central part of you, the part that chooses, into something a little different from what it was before.

C. S. LEWIS

Life is pretty much like a cafeteria line—it offers us many choices, both good and bad. The Christian must have a spiritual radar that detects the difference not only between bad and good but also among good, better, and best.

DENNIS SWANBERG

Choices can change our lives profoundly. The choice to mend a broken relationship, to say "yes" to a difficult assignment, to lay aside some important work to play with a child, to visit some forgotten person—these small choices may affect many lives eternally.

GLORIA GAITHER

We are either the masters or the victims of our attitudes. It is a matter of personal choice. Who we are today is the result of choices we made yesterday. Tomorrow, we will become what we choose today. To change means to choose to change.

JOHN MAXWELL

Faith is not a feeling; it is action. It is a willed choice.

ELISABETH ELLIOT

I do not know how the Spirit of Christ performs it, but He brings us choices through which we constantly change, fresh and new, into His likeness.

JONI EARECKSON TADA

THE TIP OF THE DAY

If you're about to make an important decision, don't be impulsive. Remember: big decisions have big consequences, and if you don't think about those consequences now, you may pay a big price later.

THE PRAYER OF THE DAY

Lord, help me to make choices that are pleasing to You.
Help me to be honest, patient, and kind.
And above all, help me to follow the teachings of Jesus,
not just today, but every day.
Amen

MY THOUGHTS ABOUT CHOICES

_____

_____

_____

_____

_____

_____

_____

DAY 21

GOD'S TIMING IS BEST

Patience and encouragement come from God.
ROMANS 15:5 NCV

YOU WILL LIVE WISELY AND WELL IF . . .
You are willing to trust God's timing in all matters,
including the timing and the nature of your relationships.

If you sincerely seek to be a woman of faith, then you must learn to trust God's timing. You will be sorely tempted, however, to do otherwise. Because you are a fallible human being, you are impatient for things to happen. But, God knows better.

God has created a world that unfolds according to His own timetable, not ours . . . thank goodness! We mortals might make a terrible mess of things. God does not.

God's plan does not always happen in the way that we would like or at the time of our own choosing. Our task—as believing Christians who trust in a benevolent, all-knowing Father—is to wait patiently for God to reveal Himself. And reveal Himself He will. Always. But until God's perfect plan is made known, we must walk in faith and never lose hope. And we must continue to trust Him. Always.

MORE FROM GOD'S WORD

*Knowing God leads to self-control. Self-control leads to patient
endurance, and patient endurance leads to godliness.*

2 PETER 1:6 NLT

Patience is better than strength.

PROVERBS 16:32 NCV

*But if we look forward to something we don't have yet, we must
wait patiently and confidently.*

ROMANS 8:25 NLT

*The Lord is wonderfully good to those who wait for him and seek
him. So it is good to wait quietly for salvation from the Lord.*

LAMENTATIONS 3:25-26 NLT

*Wait on the LORD; Be of good courage, and He shall strengthen
your heart; Wait, I say, on the LORD!*

PSALM 27:14 NKJV

MORE IDEAS ABOUT
PATIENCE AND OBEDIENCE

We cannot be led by our emotions and still be led by the Holy Spirit, so we have to make a choice.

JOYCE MEYER

The pathway of obedience can sometimes be difficult, but it always leads to a strengthening of our inner woman.

VONETTE BRIGHT

It takes faith to obey God, but God always rewards obedient faith.

WARREN WIERSBE

Obey God one step at a time, then the next step will come into view.

CATHERINE MARSHALL

Faithfulness today is the best preparation for the demands of tomorrow.

ELISABETH ELLIOT

God is more patient with us than we are with ourselves.

MAX LUCADO

In the name of Jesus Christ who was never in a hurry, we pray, O God, that You will slow us down, for we know that we live too fast. With all eternity before us, make us take time to live—time to get acquainted with You, time to enjoy Your blessing, and time to know each other.

PETER MARSHALL

THE TIP OF THE DAY

The best things in life seldom happen overnight; they usually take time. Henry Blackaby writes, "The grass that is here today and gone tomorrow does not require much time to mature. A big oak tree that lasts for generations requires much more time to grow and mature. God is concerned about your life through eternity. Allow Him to take all the time He needs to shape you for His purposes. Larger assignments will require longer periods of preparation." How true!

THE PRAYER OF THE DAY

Dear Lord, let me wait quietly for You. Let me live
according to Your plan and according to Your timetable.
When I am hurried, slow me down. When I become
impatient with others, give me empathy.
Today, I want to be a patient Christian, Lord,
as I trust in You and in Your master plan.
Amen

MY THOUGHTS ABOUT
PATIENCE AND OBEDIENCE

_____

_____

_____

_____

_____

_____

_____

_____

DAY 22

ADDICTIONS 101

You shall have no other gods before Me.

Exodus 20:3 NKJV

YOU WILL LIVE WISELY AND WELL IF . . .
You recognize the dangers of addiction
and behave accordingly.

ddictions and righteousness don't mix. Yet ours is a society that glamorizes the use of drugs, alcohol, cigarettes, and other addictive substances.

The dictionary defines *addiction* as "the compulsive need for a habit-forming substance; the condition of being habitually and compulsively occupied with something." That definition is accurate but incomplete. For Christians, addiction has an additional meaning: it means compulsively worshipping something other than God.

Unless you're living on a deserted island, you know people who are full-blown addicts—probably lots of people. If you, or someone you love, is suffering from the blight of addiction, remember this: Help is available. Many people have experienced addiction and lived to tell about it . . . so don't give up hope.

And if you're one of those fortunate people who hasn't started experimenting with addictive substances, congratulations! You have just spared yourself a lifetime of headaches and heartaches.

MORE FROM GOD'S WORD

*Be sober! Be on the alert! Your adversary the Devil is prowling
around like a roaring lion, looking for anyone he can devour.*

1 PETER 5:8 HCSB

*This High Priest of ours understands our weaknesses, for he faced
all of the same temptations we do, yet he did not sin.*

HEBREWS 4:15 NLT

*Jesus responded, "I assure you: Everyone who commits sin is a slave
of sin."*

JOHN 8:34 HCSB

*Death is the reward of an undisciplined life; your foolish decisions
trap you in a dead end.*

PROVERBS 5:23 MSG

*If they serve Him obediently, they will end their days in prosperity
and their years in happiness.*

JOB 36:11 HCSB

MORE IDEAS ABOUT ADDICTION

Addiction is the most powerful psychic enemy of humanity's desire for God.

GERALD MAY

We are meant to be addicted to God, but we develop secondary additions that temporarily appear to fix our problem.

EDWARD M. BERCKMAN

Above all, we must be especially alert against the beginnings of temptation, for the enemy is more easily conquered if he is refused admittance to the mind and is met beyond the threshold when he knocks.

THOMAS À KEMPIS

The drunken man is a living corpse.

ST. JOHN CHRYSOSTOM

The soul that journeys to God, but doesn't shake off its cares and quiet its appetites, is like someone who drags a cart uphill.

ST. JOHN OF THE CROSS

A spiritual discipline is necessary in order to move slowly from an absurd to an obedient life, from a life filled with noisy worries to a life in which there is some free inner space where we can listen to our God and follow his guidance.

HENRI NOUWEN

God cannot build character without our cooperation. If we resist Him, then He chastens us into submission. But, if we submit to Him, then He can accomplish His work. He is not satisfied with a halfway job. God wants a perfect work; He wants a finished product that is mature and complete.

WARREN WIERSBE

The alternative to discipline is disaster.

VANCE HAVNER

THE TIP OF THE DAY
Guard your heart against addiction . . . or else.

THE PRAYER OF THE DAY

Dear Lord, You have instructed me to care for my body,
and I will obey You. I will be mindful of the destructive
power of addiction, and I will avoid the people,
the places, and the substances that can entrap
my spirit and destroy my life.

Amen

MY THOUGHTS ABOUT
ADDICTION

_____

_____

_____

_____

_____

_____

_____

DAY 23

THE RIGHT KIND OF PRIORITIES

Steep your life in God-reality, God-initiative, God-provisions.
Don't worry about missing out. You'll find all your everyday
human concerns will be met.

MATTHEW 6:33 MSG

YOU WILL LIVE WISELY AND WELL IF . . .
You establish priorities that are pleasing to God.

First things first. These words are easy to speak but hard to put into practice. For busy women living in a demanding world, placing first things first can be difficult indeed. Why? Because so many people are expecting so many things from us!

If you're having trouble prioritizing your day, perhaps you've been trying to organize your life according to your own plans, not God's. A better strategy, of course, is to take your daily obligations and place them in the hands of the One who created you. To do so, you must prioritize your day according to God's commandments, and you must seek His will and His wisdom in all matters. Then, you can face the day with the assurance that the same God who created our universe out of nothingness will help you place first things first in your own life.

Do you feel overwhelmed or confused? Turn the concerns of this day over to God—prayerfully, earnestly, and often. Then listen for His answer . . . and trust the answer He gives.

MORE FROM GOD'S WORD

First pay attention to me, and then relax. Now you can take it easy–you're in good hands.

PROVERBS 1:33 MSG

And I pray this: that your love will keep on growing in knowledge and every kind of discernment, so that you can determine what really matters and can be pure and blameless in the day of Christ.

PHILIPPIANS 1:9 HCSB

Let us fix our eyes on Jesus, the author and perfecter of our faith, who for the joy set before him endured the cross, scorning its shame, and sat down at the right hand of the throne of God.

HEBREWS 12:2 NIV

But Martha was pulled away by all she had to do in the kitchen. Later, she stepped in, interrupting them. "Master, don't you care that my sister has abandoned the kitchen to me? Tell her to lend me a hand." The Master said, "Martha, dear Martha, you're fussing far too much and getting yourself worked up over nothing. One thing only is essential, and Mary has chosen it–it's the main course, and won't be taken from her."

LUKE 10:40-42 MSG

MORE IDEAS ABOUT PRIORITIES

The things that matter most in this world can never be held in your hand.

GLORIA GAITHER

It's sobering to contemplate how much time, effort, sacrifice, compromise, and attention we give to acquiring and increasing our supply of something that is totally insignificant in eternity.

ANNE GRAHAM LOTZ

Great relief and satisfaction can come from seeking God's priorities for us in each season, discerning what is "best" in the midst of many noble opportunities, and pouring our most excellent energies into those things.

BETH MOORE

Sin is largely a matter of mistaken priorities. Any sin in us that is cherished, hidden, and not confessed will cut the nerve center of our faith.

CATHERINE MARSHALL

Getting things accomplished isn't nearly as important as taking time for love.

JANETTE OKE

There were endless demands on Jesus' time. Still he was able to make that amazing claim of "completing the work you gave me to do." (John 17:4 NIV)

ELISABETH ELLIOT

Have you prayed about your resources lately? Find out how God wants you to use your time and your money. No matter what it costs, forsake all that is not of God.

KAY ARTHUR

THE TIP OF THE DAY

Make God a priority: Your days are probably filled to the brim with lots of obligations. But remember: no obligation is greater than the debt you owe to your Creator. So make sure that you give Him the time He deserves, not only on Sundays, but also on every other day of the week. Anne Graham Lotz observes, "It's sobering to contemplate how much time, effort, sacrifice, compromise, and attention we give to acquiring and increasing our supply of something that is totally insignificant in eternity." Plan your day—and your life—accordingly.

THE PRAYER OF THE DAY

Lord, let Your priorities be my priorities.
Let Your will be my will. Let Your Word be my guide,
and let me grow in faith and in wisdom
this day and every day.
Amen

MY THOUGHTS ABOUT
PRIORITIES

_____

_____

_____

_____

_____

_____

_____

DAY 24

YOUR FAMILY IS GOD'S GIFT TO YOU

*Their first responsibility is to show godliness at home
and repay their parents by taking care of them.
This is something that pleases God very much.*

1 TIMOTHY 5:4 NLT

YOU WILL LIVE WISELY AND WELL IF . . .
You build a strong bridge between yourself and your family.

O kay, it's official: you're a busy young woman with lots of places to go, lots of things to do, and plenty of stuff to see. And you're probably in a hurry to get going. But as you consider God's purpose for your own life, you must also consider how your plans will effect the most important people that God has entrusted to your care: your loved ones.

A loving family is a treasure from God. If you happen to be a member of a close knit, supportive clan, offer a word of thanks to your Creator. He has blessed you with one of His most precious earthly possessions. Your obligation, in response to God's gift, is to treat your family in ways that are consistent with His commandments.

God intends that we honor Him by honoring our families. We honor our families by giving them our love, our support, our consideration, and our cooperation. Make no mistake: these matters require significant investments of time.

No family is perfect, and neither is yours. Yet in spite of the inevitable challenges of family life, your clan is God's gift to you. That little band of men, women, kids, and babies comprises a priceless treasure on temporary loan from the Father above. It's up to you to act—and to plan— accordingly.

MORE FROM GOD'S WORD

You must choose for yourselves today whom you will serve . . . as for me and my family, we will serve the Lord.

JOSHUA 24:15 NCV

Love must be without hypocrisy. Detest evil; cling to what is good. Show family affection to one another with brotherly love. Outdo one another in showing honor.

ROMANS 12:9-10 HCSB

Let love and faithfulness never leave you . . . write them on the tablet of your heart.

PROVERBS 3:3 NIV

If a kingdom is divided against itself, that kingdom cannot stand. If a house is divided against itself, that house cannot stand.

MARK 3:24-25 HCSB

Unless the Lord builds a house, its builders labor over it in vain; unless the Lord watches over a city, the watchman stays alert in vain.

PSALM 127:1 HSCB

MORE IDEAS ABOUT FAMILY

A home is a place where we find direction.

GIGI GRAHAM TCHIVIDJIAN

When you think about it for a moment, it certainly makes sense that if people can establish a loving and compatible relationship at home, they have a better chance of establishing winning relationships with those with whom they work on a regular basis.

ZIG ZIGLAR

Living life with a consistent spiritual walk deeply influences those we love most.

VONETTE BRIGHT

My primary role is not to be the boss and just look good, but to be a servant leader who enables and enhances my family to be their best.

TIM HANSEL

Creating a warm, caring, supportive, encouraging environment is probably the most important thing you can do for your family.

STEPHEN COVEY

When God asks someone to do something for Him entailing sacrifice, he makes up for it in surprising ways. Though He has led Bill all over the world to preach the gospel, He has not forgotten the little family in the mountains of North Carolina.

RUTH BELL GRAHAM

The only true source of meaning in life is found in love for God and his son Jesus Christ, and love for mankind, beginning with our own families.

JAMES DOBSON

There is so much compassion and understanding that is gained when we've experienced God's grace firsthand within our own families.

LISA WHELCHEL

THE TIP OF THE DAY

No matter how busy you are . . . make time for your family. You'll be blessed and so will they. Chuck Swindoll has simple advice: "Never give your family the leftovers and crumbs of your time." And he's right.

THE PRAYER OF THE DAY

Dear Lord, You have given me a wonderful gift:
a loving family. Today and every day, let me show
my family that I love them by the things
that I say and the things that I do.
Amen

MY THOUGHTS ABOUT FAMILY

_____

_____

_____

_____

_____

_____

_____

DAY 25

YOU'RE
AN EXAMPLE . . .
BE A GOOD ONE

*You should be an example to the believers in speech,
in conduct, in love, in faith, in purity.*
1 Timothy 4:12 HCSB

YOU WILL LIVE WISELY AND WELL IF . . .
You find good examples to follow, and if you're determined
to be a good example, too.

Whether we like it or not, all of us are role models. Our friends and family members watch our actions and, as followers of Christ, we are obliged to act accordingly.

What kind of example are you? Are you the kind of person whose life serves as a genuine example of righteousness? Are you a woman whose behavior serves as a positive role model for others? Are you the kind of person whose actions, day in and day out, are based upon kindness, faithfulness, and a love for the Lord? If so, you are not only blessed by God, you are also a powerful force for good in a world that desperately needs positive influences such as yours.

We live in a dangerous, temptation-filled world. That's why you encounter so many opportunities to stray from God's commandments. Resist those temptations! When you do, you'll earn God's blessings and you'll serve as a positive role model for your family and friends.

Corrie ten Boom advised, "Don't worry about what you do not understand. Worry about what you do understand in the Bible but do not live by." And that's sound advice because our families and friends are watching . . . and so, for that matter, is God.

MORE FROM GOD'S WORD

In everything you do, stay away from complaining and arguing, so that no one can speak a word of blame against you. You are to live clean, innocent lives as children of God in a dark world full of crooked and perverse people. Let your lives shine brightly before them.

PHILIPPIANS 2:14-15 NLT

You are the light that gives light to the world . . . . In the same way, you should be a light for other people. Live so that they will see the good things you do and will praise your Father in heaven.

MATTHEW 5:14, 16 NCV

Do you want to be counted wise, to build a reputation for wisdom? Here's what you do: Live well, live wisely, live humbly. It's the way you live, not the way you talk, that counts.

JAMES 3:13 MSG

We're Christ's representatives. God uses us to persuade men and women to drop their differences and enter into God's work of making things right between them. We're speaking for Christ himself now: Become friends with God; he's already a friend with you.

2 CORINTHIANS 5:20 MSG

MORE IDEAS ABOUT EXAMPLE

Among the most joyful people I have known have been some who seem to have had no human reason for joy. The sweet fragrance of Christ has shown through their lives.

ELISABETH ELLIOT

In serving we uncover the greatest fulfillment within and become a stellar example of a woman who knows and loves Jesus.

VONETTE BRIGHT

A person who lives right, and is right, has more power in his silence than another has by words.

PHILLIPS BROOKS

Nothing speaks louder or more powerfully than a life of integrity.

CHARLES SWINDOLL

Your life will not convince those around you of the reality of Jesus if you cannot live in unity with your fellow Christians.

HENRY BLACKABY

In your desire to share the gospel, you may be the only Jesus someone else will ever meet. Be real and be involved with people.

BARBARA JOHNSON

Our walk counts far more than our talk, always!

GEORGE MUELLER

The religion of Jesus Christ has an ethical as well as a doctrinal side.

LOTTIE MOON

THE TIP OF THE DAY

Follow a good example and be a good example. Max Lucado writes, "In our faith we follow in someone's steps. In our faith we leave footprints to guide others. It's the principle of discipleship." Remember: It's not enough to talk about being a Christian; you must also show other people that you're a disciple of Christ.

THE PRAYER OF THE DAY

Dear Lord, help me be a worthy example to my friends
and to my family. Let the things that I say
and the things that I do show everyone what it means
to be a follower of Your Son.
Amen

MY THOUGHTS ABOUT
EXAMPLE

_____

_____

_____

_____

_____

_____

_____

DAY 26

GOD HAS A PLAN FOR YOU

The Lord says, "I will guide you along the best pathway for your life. I will advise you and watch over you."

PSALM 32:8 NLT

YOU WILL LIVE WISELY AND WELL IF . . .
You genuinely seek God's plan for your life . . .
and if you follow it.

You've probably heard the song "My Way" (it was Frank Sinatra's theme song, and Elvis sang it, too). "My Way" is a perfectly good tune, but it's not a perfect guide for life-here-on-earth. If you're looking for life's perfect prescription—if you're looking for joy, peace, abundance, and eternal life—you'd better forget about doing things your way and start doing things God's way.

God has plans for your life. Big plans. But He won't force you to follow His will; to the contrary, He has given you free will, the ability to make decisions on your own. With the freedom to choose comes the responsibility of living with the consequences of the choices you make.

The most important decision of your life is, of course, your commitment to accept Jesus Christ as your personal Lord and Savior. And once your eternal destiny is secured, you will undoubtedly ask yourself the question "What now, Lord?" If you earnestly seek God's will for your life, you will find it . . . in time.

Sometimes, God's plans are crystal clear, but other times, He leads us through the wilderness before He delivers us to the Promised Land. So be patient, keep searching, and keep praying. If you do, then in time, God will answer your prayers and make His plans known.

God is right here, and He intends to use you in wonderful, unexpected ways. You'll discover those plans by doing things His way . . . and you'll be eternally grateful that you did.

MORE FROM GOD'S WORD

The true children of God are those who let God's Spirit lead them.

ROMANS 8:14 NCV

Lord, You light my lamp; my God illuminates my darkness.

PSALM 18:28 HCSB

In all your ways acknowledge Him, and He shall direct your paths.

PROVERBS 3:6 NKJV

"For I know the plans I have for you," declares the Lord, "plans to prosper you and not to harm you, plans to give you hope and a future. Then you will call upon me and come and pray to me, and I will listen to you."

JEREMIAH 29:11-12 NIV

I know that You can do anything and no plan of Yours can be thwarted.

JOB 42:2 HCSB

MORE IDEAS ABOUT
GOD'S PLANS

When the dream of our heart is one that God has planted there, a strange happiness flows into us. At that moment, all of the spiritual resources of the universe are released to help us. Our praying is then at one with the will of God and becomes a channel for the Creator's purposes for us and our world.

CATHERINE MARSHALL

All God's plans have the mark of the cross on them, and all His plans have death to self in them.

E. M. BOUNDS

It's incredible to realize that what we do each day has meaning in the big picture of God's plan.

BILL HYBELS

The one supreme business of life is to find God's plan for your life and live it.

E. STANLEY JONES

God has a plan for the life of every Christian. Every circumstance, every turn of destiny, all things work together for your good and for His glory.

BILLY GRAHAM

We will stand amazed to see the topside of the tapestry and how God beautifully embroidered each circumstance into a pattern for our good and His glory.

JONI EARECKSON TADA

God surrounds you with opportunity. You and I are free in Jesus Christ, not to do whatever we want, but to be all that God wants us to be.

WARREN WIERSBE

THE TIP OF THE DAY

God has a perfect plan for your life. Gloria Gaither writes, "With God, it's never 'Plan B' or 'second best.' It's always 'Plan A.' And, if we let Him, He'll make something beautiful of our lives." God can make your life beautiful; your job is to let Him do it.

THE PRAYER OF THE DAY

Dear Lord, You have a wonderful plan for my life.
Let me discover it, trust it, and follow it so that I can
become the person You want me to become.

Amen

MY THOUGHTS ABOUT
GOD'S PLANS

_____

_____

_____

_____

_____

_____

_____

_____

DAY 27

KNOWING HIS TRUTH AND LIVING BY IT

Then you will know the truth, and the truth will set you free.

JOHN 8:32 NIV

YOU WILL LIVE WISELY AND WELL IF . . .
You keep searching for the Truth with a capital T.

God is vitally concerned with truth. His Word teaches the truth; His Spirit reveals the truth; His Son leads us to the truth. When we open our hearts to God, and when we allow His Son to rule over our thoughts and our lives, God reveals Himself, and we come to understand the truth about ourselves and the Truth (with a capital T) about God's gift of grace.

The familiar words of John 8:32 remind us that when we come to know God's Truth, we are liberated. Have you been liberated by that Truth? And are you living in accordance with the eternal truths that you find in God's Holy Word? Hopefully so.

Today, as you fulfill the responsibilities that God has placed before you, ask yourself this question: "Do my thoughts and actions bear witness to the ultimate Truth that God has placed in my heart, or am I allowing the pressures of everyday life to overwhelm me?" It's a profound question that deserves an answer . . . now.

MORE FROM GOD'S WORD

Jesus said to him, "I am the way, the truth, and the life. No one comes to the Father except through Me. If you had known Me, you would have known My Father also; and from now on you know Him and have seen Him."

JOHN 14:6-7 NKJV

Be diligent to present yourself approved to God, a worker who doesn't need to be ashamed, correctly teaching the word of truth.

2 TIMOTHY 2:15 HCSB

When the Spirit of truth comes, He will guide you into all the truth.

JOHN 16:13 HCSB

Therefore laying aside falsehood, speak truth, each one of you, with his neighbor, for we are members of one another.

EPHESIANS 4:25 NASB

You have already heard about this hope in the message of truth, the gospel that has come to you. It is bearing fruit and growing all over the world, just as it has among you since the day you heard it and recognized God's grace in the truth.

COLOSSIANS 1:5-6 HCSB

MORE IDEAS ABOUT TRUTH

The difficult truth about truth is that it often requires us to change our perspectives, attitudes, and rules for living.

SUSAN LENZKES

For Christians, God himself is the only absolute; truth and ethics are rooted in his character.

CHUCK COLSON

Peace, if possible, but truth at any rate.

MARTIN LUTHER

To worship Him in truth means to worship Him honestly, without hypocrisy, standing open and transparent before Him.

ANNE GRAHAM LOTZ

Having a doctrine pass before the mind is not what the Bible means by knowing the truth. It's only when it reaches down deep into the heart that the truth begins to set us free, just as a key must penetrate a lock to turn it, or as rainfall must saturate the earth down to the roots in order for your garden to grow.

JOHN ELDREDGE

Jesus differs from all other teachers; they reach the ear, but he instructs the heart; they deal with the outward letter, but he imparts an inward taste for the truth.

C. H. SPURGEON

The Holy Spirit was given to guide us into all truth, but He doesn't do it all at once.

ELISABETH ELLIOT

The only people who achieve much are those who want knowledge so badly that they seek it while the conditions are still unfavorable. Favorable conditions never come.

C. S. LEWIS

THE TIP OF THE DAY

Warren Wiersbe writes, "Learning God's truth and getting it into our heads is one thing, but living God's truth and getting it into our characters is quite something else." So don't be satisfied to sit on the sidelines and observe the truth at a distance—live it.

THE PRAYER OF THE DAY

Heavenly Father, You are the way and the truth
and the light. Today—as I follow Your way and share
Your Good News—let me be a worthy example to others
and a worthy servant to You.

Amen

MY THOUGHTS ABOUT
TRUTH

_____

_____

_____

_____

_____

_____

_____

DAY 28

DON'T WORRY TOO MUCH ABOUT PLEASING PEOPLE ... PLEASE GOD

Do you think I am trying to make people accept me?
No, God is the One I am trying to please.
Am I trying to please people? If I still wanted to please people,
I would not be a servant of Christ.

GALATIANS 1:10 NCV

YOU WILL LIVE WISELY AND WELL IF ...
You learn to recognize and resist negative peer pressure.

Rick Warren observed, "Those who follow the crowd usually get lost in it." We know these words to be true, but oftentimes we fail to live by them. Instead of trusting God for guidance, we imitate our friends and suffer the consequences. Instead of seeking to please our Father in heaven, we strive to please our peers, with decidedly mixed results.

Would you like a time-tested formula for successful living? Here is a formula that is proven and true: Seek God's approval first and other people's approval later. Does this sound too simple? Perhaps it is simple, but it is also the only way to reap the marvelous riches that God has in store for you.

Whom will you try to please today: your God or your friends? Your obligation is most certainly not to friends or even to family members. Your obligation is to an all-knowing, all-powerful God. You must seek to please Him first and always. No exceptions.

MORE FROM GOD'S WORD

My dear friends, don't let public opinion influence how you live out our glorious, Christ-originated faith.

JAMES 2:1 MSG

He said to them, "You make yourselves look good in front of people, but God knows what is really in your hearts. What is important to people is hateful in God's sight.

LUKE 16:15 NCV

Don't be selfish; don't live to make a good impression on others.

PHILIPPIANS 2:3 NLT

My son, if sinners entice you, don't be persuaded.

PROVERBS 1:10 HCSB

Blessed is the man who walks not in the counsel of the ungodly, nor stands in the path of sinners, nor sits in the seat of the scornful; but his delight is in the law of the Lord, and in His law he meditates day and night.

PSALM 1:1-2 NKJV

MORE IDEAS ABOUT PEER PRESSURE

It is comfortable to know that we are responsible to God and not to man. It is a small matter to be judged of man's judgement.

LOTTIE MOON

We, as God's people, are not only to stay far away from sin and sinners who would entice us, but we are to be so like our God that we mourn over sin.

KAY ARTHUR

You will get untold flak for prioritizing God's revealed and present will for your life over man's . . . but, boy, is it worth it.

BETH MOORE

Comparison is the root of all feelings of inferiority.

JAMES DOBSON

There is nothing that makes more cowards and feeble men than public opinion.

HENRY WARD BEECHER

True friends will always lift you higher and challenge you to walk in a manner pleasing to our Lord.

LISA BEVERE

For better or worse, you will eventually become more and more like the people you associate with. So why not associate with people who make you better, not worse?

MARIE T. FREEMAN

I have found that the closer I am to the godly people around me, the easier it is for me to live a righteous life because they hold me accountable.

JOHN MACARTHUR

THE TIP OF THE DAY

Don't worry about popularity contests. When you have a choice between pleasing others and pleasing God, choose God.

THE PRAYER OF THE DAY

Dear Lord, today I will worry less about pleasing other
people and more about pleasing You. I will stand up for
my beliefs, and I will honor You with my thoughts,
my actions, and my prayers. And I will worship You, Father,
with thanksgiving in my heart, this day and forever.

Amen

MY THOUGHTS ABOUT
PEER PRESSURE

_____

_____

_____

_____

_____

_____

_____

DAY 29

GOD WANTS YOU TO FOCUS ON THE RIGHT THINGS

*Keep your eyes focused on what is right,
and look straight ahead to what is good.*

PROVERBS 4:25 NCV

YOU WILL LIVE WISELY AND WELL IF . . .
You focus your thoughts and your energies
on God's will for your life.

What is your focus today? Are you willing to focus your thoughts and energies on God's blessings and upon His will for your life? Or will you turn your thoughts to other things? Before you answer that question, consider this: God created you in His own image, and He wants you to experience joy and abundance. But, God will not insist that you experience His joy; you must claim it for yourself.

This day—and every day hereafter—is a chance to celebrate the life that God has given you. It's also a chance to give thanks to the One who has offered you more blessings than you can possibly count.

Today, why not focus your thoughts on the joy that is rightfully yours in Christ? Why not take time to celebrate God's glorious creation? Why not focus on the blessings that God bestows upon those who obey Him and honor Him? When you do, you will think optimistically about yourself and your world . . . and you can then share your optimism with others. They'll be better for it, and so will you. But not necessarily in that order.

MORE FROM GOD'S WORD

In everything set them an example by doing what is good.

TITUS 2:7 NIV

Are there those among you who are truly wise and understanding? Then they should show it by living right and doing good things with a gentleness that comes from wisdom.

JAMES 3:13 NCV

Even a child is known by his actions, by whether his conduct is pure and right.

PROVERBS 20:11 NIV

God hasn't invited us into a disorderly, unkempt life but into something holy and beautiful—as beautiful on the inside as the outside.

1 THESSALONIANS 4:7 MSG

So let's keep focused on that goal, those of us who want everything God has for us. If any of you have something else in mind, something less than total commitment, God will clear your blurred vision—you'll see it yet! Now that we're on the right track, let's stay on it.

PHILIPPIANS 3:15-16 MSG

MORE IDEAS ABOUT FOCUS

Measure the size of the obstacles against the size of God.

BETH MOORE

We need to stop focusing on our lacks and stop giving out excuses and start looking at and listening to Jesus.

ANNE GRAHAM LOTZ

Setting goals is one way you can be sure that you will focus your efforts on the main things so that trivial matters will not become your focus.

CHARLES STANLEY

Whatever we focus on determines what we become.

E. STANLEY JONES

Paul did one thing. Most of us dabble in forty things. Are you a doer or a dabbler?

VANCE HAVNER

Forgetting your mission leads, inevitably, to getting tangled up in details—details that can take you completely off your path.

LAURIE BETH JONES

One can get just as much exultation in losing oneself in a little thing as in a big thing. It is nice to think how one can be recklessly lost in a daisy!

ANNE MORROW LINDBERGH

Just like commercial organizations need to get their focus off themselves, we as individual Christians and collective churches need to recalibrate our sights on the target God has given us: spiritually lost people.

BILL HYBELS

THE TIP OF THE DAY

Ask yourself if you're truly focusing your thoughts and energies on matters that are pleasing to God. Then ask your Creator to help you focus on His love, His Son, and His plan for your life.

THE PRAYER OF THE DAY

Lord, I pray for an attitude that is Christlike.
Whatever my circumstances, whether good or bad,
triumphal or tragic, let my response reflect a God-honoring
attitude of optimism, faith, and love for You.

Amen

MY THOUGHTS ABOUT
FOCUS

_____

_____

_____

_____

_____

_____

_____

DAY 30

YOUR DAILY DEVOTIONAL

Every morning he wakes me. He teaches me to listen like a student. The Lord God helps me learn . . . .

ISAIAH 50:4-5 NCV

YOU WILL LIVE WISELY AND WELL IF . . .

You make it a habit to talk to God
first thing every morning.

When it comes to spending time with God, are you a "squeezer" or a "pleaser"? Do you squeeze God into your busy schedule with an occasional prayer before meals (and maybe with a quick visit to church on Sunday)? Or do you please God by talking to Him far more often than that? If you're wise, you'll form the habit of spending time with God every day. When you do, it will change your life.

When you begin each day with your head bowed and your heart lifted, you remind yourself of God's love, His protection, and His commandments. And if you are wise, you will use your morning prayer time to align your priorities for the coming day with the teachings and commandments of God's Holy Word.

Are you seeking the abundance and joy that can be yours through Christ? Do you seek to improve the condition of your spiritual or physical health? If so, ask for God's help and ask for it many times each day . . . starting with your morning devotional.

MORE FROM GOD'S WORD

Let the words of my mouth and the meditation of my heart be acceptable in Your sight, O Lord, my strength and my Redeemer.

PSALM 19:14 NKJV

It is good to give thanks to the Lord, to sing praises to the Most High. It is good to proclaim your unfailing love in the morning, your faithfulness in the evening.

PSALM 92:1-2 NLT

But grow in the grace and knowledge of our Lord and Savior Jesus Christ. To Him be the glory both now and to the day of eternity.

2 PETER 3:18 HCSB

Praise the Lord! Oh, give thanks to the Lord, for He is good! For His mercy endures forever.

PSALM 106:1 NKJV

So that at the name of Jesus every knee should bow—of those who are in heaven and on earth and under the earth—and every tongue should confess that Jesus Christ is Lord, to the glory of God the Father.

PHILIPPIANS 2:10-11 HCSB

MORE IDEAS ABOUT DAILY DEVOTIONALS

How motivating it has been for me to view my early morning devotions as time of retreat alone with Jesus, Who desires that I "come with Him by myself to a quiet place" in order to pray, read His Word, listen for His voice, and be renewed in my spirit.

ANNE GRAHAM LOTZ

Make a plan now to keep a daily appointment with God. The enemy is going to tell you to set it aside, but you must carve out the time. If you're too busy to meet with the Lord, friend, then you are simply too busy.

CHARLES SWINDOLL

Surrender your mind to the Lord at the beginning of each day.

WARREN WIERSBE

If we really believe not only that God exists but also that God is actively present in our lives—healing, teaching, and guiding—we need to set aside a time and space to give God our undivided attention.

HENRI NOUWEN

God is a place of safety you can run to, but it helps if you are running to Him on a daily basis so that you are in familiar territory.

STORMIE OMARTIAN

We must appropriate the tender mercy of God every day after conversion or problems quickly develop. We need his grace daily in order to live a righteous life.

JIM CYMBALA

Our devotion to God is strengthened when we offer Him a fresh commitment each day.

ELIZABETH GEORGE

THE TIP OF THE DAY

Find the best time of the day to spend with God: Hudson Taylor, an English missionary, wrote, "Whatever is your best time in the day, give that to communion with God." That's powerful advice that leads to a powerful faith.

THE PRAYER OF THE DAY

Lord, help me to hear Your direction for my life
in the quiet moments of each day. Let everything
that I say and do be in Your perfect will.

Amen

MY THOUGHTS ABOUT
DAILY DEVOTIONALS

_____

_____

_____

_____

_____

_____

_____

_____

DAY 31

THE TIME TO ACCEPT GOD'S GRACE IS NOW

But God, who is abundant in mercy, because of His great love that
He had for us, made us alive with the Messiah even though we
were dead in trespasses. By grace you are saved!

EPHESIANS 2:4-5 HCSB

YOU WILL LIVE WISELY AND WELL IF . . .

You don't miss out on God's gifts:
Every day is a beautifully wrapped gift from God.
Unwrap it, and give thanks to the Giver.

Jesus is the spiritual sun that gives warmth, light, and life to the world. Christ died on the cross so that we might have eternal life. This gift, freely given from God's only Son, is the priceless possession of everyone who accepts Him as Lord and Savior.

Thankfully, God's grace is not an earthly reward for righteous behavior; it is, instead, a blessed spiritual gift. When we accept Christ into our hearts, we are saved by His grace.

God's grace is the ultimate gift, and we owe Him our eternal gratitude. Our Heavenly Father is waiting patiently for each of us to accept His Son and receive His grace. Let us accept that gift today so that we might enjoy God's presence now and throughout all eternity.

MORE FROM GOD'S WORD

My grace is sufficient for you, for My strength is made perfect in weakness.

2 CORINTHIANS 12:9 NKJV

For by grace you are saved through faith, and this is not from yourselves; it is God's gift—not from works, so that no one can boast.

EPHESIANS 2:8-9 HCSB

And we have seen and testify that the Father has sent the Son as Savior of the world.

1 JOHN 4:14 NKJV

For if, by the trespass of the one man, death reigned through that one man, how much more will those who receive God's abundant provision of grace and of the gift of righteousness reign in life through the one man, Jesus Christ.

ROMANS 5:17 NIV

For God so loved the world, that he gave his only begotten Son, that whosoever believeth in him should not perish, but have everlasting life.

JOHN 3:16 KJV

MORE IDEAS ABOUT
GOD'S GRACE AND ETERNAL LIFE

Your choice to either receive or reject the Lord Jesus Christ
will determine where you spend eternity.

ANNE GRAHAM LOTZ

If you are a believer, your judgment will not determine
your eternal destiny. Christ's finished work on Calvary was
applied to you the moment you accepted Christ as Savior.

BETH MOORE

The damage done to us on this earth will never find its way
into that safe city. We can relax, we can rest, and though
some of us can hardly imagine it, we can prepare to feel safe
and secure for all of eternity.

BILL HYBELS

God has promised us abundance, peace, and eternal life.
These treasures are ours for the asking; all we must do is
claim them. One of the great mysteries of life is why on
earth do so many of us wait so very long to lay claim to
God's gifts?

MARIE T. FREEMAN

It is in giving that we receive, it is in pardoning that we are pardoned, it is in dying that we are born to eternal life.

ST. FRANCIS

And because we know Christ is alive, we have hope for the present and hope for life beyond the grave.

BILLY GRAHAM

Teach us to set our hopes on heaven, to hold firmly to the promise of eternal life, so that we can withstand the struggles and storms of this world.

MAX LUCADO

THE TIP OF THE DAY

God offers you life abundant and life eternal. If you have not accepted His gift, the appropriate moment to do so is now.

THE PRAYER OF THE DAY

Lord, You have saved me by Your grace and You sustain me
by Your grace. Keep me mindful that Your grace is a gift
that I can accept but cannot earn. I praise You
for that priceless gift, today and forever.

Amen

MY THOUGHTS ABOUT
GOD'S GRACE AND ETERNAL LIFE

_____

_____

_____

_____

_____

_____

_____

_____

BIBLE VERSES
TO CONSIDER

WISDOM

Do not deceive yourselves. If any one of you thinks he is wise by the standards of this age, he should become a "fool" so that he may become wise. For the wisdom of this world is foolishness in God's sight.

1 CORINTHIANS 3:18-19 NIV

But if any of you lacks wisdom, let him ask of God, who gives to all generously and without reproach, and it will be given to him.

JAMES 1:5 NASB

The wisdom that is from above is first pure, then peaceable, gentle, and easy to be entreated, full of mercy and good fruits, without partiality, and without hypocrisy.

JAMES 3:17 KJV

Reverence for the Lord is the foundation of true wisdom. The rewards of wisdom come to all who obey him.

PSALM 111:10 NLT

I WILL INSTRUCT YOU
AND TEACH YOU IN THE WAY
YOU SHOULD GO;
I WILL COUNSEL YOU
AND WATCH OVER YOU.

—

PSALM 32:8 NIV

COURAGE

Be strong and courageous, and do the work. Don't be afraid or discouraged, for the Lord God, my God, is with you. He won't leave you or forsake you.

1 CHRONICLES 28:20 HCSB

For God has not given us a spirit of fearfulness, but one of power, love, and sound judgment.

2 TIMOTHY 1:7 HCSB

Haven't I commanded you: be strong and courageous? Do not be afraid or discouraged, for the Lord your God is with you wherever you go.

JOSHUA 1:9 HCSB

But when Jesus heard it, He answered him, "Don't be afraid. Only believe."

LUKE 8:50 HCSB

BE ALERT, STAND FIRM
IN THE FAITH,
BE BRAVE AND STRONG.

–

1 CORINTHIANS 16:13 HCSB

ATTITUDE

There is one thing I always do. Forgetting the past and straining toward what is ahead, I keep trying to reach the goal and get the prize for which God called me . . . .

PHILIPPIANS 3:13–14 NCV

Keep your eyes focused on what is right, and look straight ahead to what is good.

PROVERBS 4:25 NCV

A miserable heart means a miserable life; a cheerful heart fills the day with a song.

PROVERBS 15:15 MSG

You were taught, with regard to your former way of life, to put off your old self, which is being corrupted by its deceitful desires; to be made new in the attitude of your minds; and to put on the new self, created to be like God in true righteousness and holiness.

EPHESIANS 4:22-24 NIV

FOR GOD HAS NOT GIVEN US
A SPIRIT OF FEAR,
BUT OF POWER AND OF LOVE
AND OF A SOUND MIND.

–

2 TIMOTHY 1:7 NLT

GOD'S LOVE

For God loved the world in this way: He gave His only Son, so that everyone who believes in Him will not perish but have eternal life.

JOHN 3:16 HCSB

For the Lord is good, and His love is eternal; His faithfulness endures through all generations.

PSALM 100:5 HCSB

[Because of] the Lord's faithful love we do not perish, for His mercies never end. They are new every morning; great is Your faithfulness!

LAMENTATIONS 3:22-23 HCSB

Whoever is wise will observe these things, and they will understand the lovingkindness of the Lord.

PSALM 107:43 NKJV

HELP ME, LORD MY GOD;
SAVE ME ACCORDING
TO YOUR FAITHFUL LOVE.

–

PSALM 109:26 HCSB

HAPPINESS

I've learned by now to be quite content whatever my circumstances. I'm just as happy with little as with much, with much as with little. I've found the recipe for being happy whether full or hungry, hands full or hands empty.

PHILIPPIANS 4:11-12 MSG

I will praise you, Lord, with all my heart. I will tell all the miracles you have done. I will be happy because of you; God Most High, I will sing praises to your name.

PSALM 9:1-2 NCV

How happy are those who can live in your house, always singing your praises. How happy are those who are strong in the Lord . . . .

PSALM 84:4-5 NLT

A happy heart makes the face cheerful, but heartache crushes the spirit.

PROVERBS 15:13 NIV

A CHEERFUL HEART IS GOOD MEDICINE . . . .

–

PROVERBS 17:22 NIV

MAN DOES NOT SEE WHAT
THE LORD SEES,
FOR MAN SEES WHAT IS VISIBLE,
BUT THE LORD SEES
THE HEART.

—

1 SAMUEL 16:7 HCSB